Matthew M. Vriends, PhD

Conures

Everything About Purchase, Housing, Care,
Nutrition, Breeding, and Diseases

With a Special Chapter on Understanding Conures

With 24 Color Photographs
41 illustrations by Tanya M. Vriends
and Michele Earle-Bridges

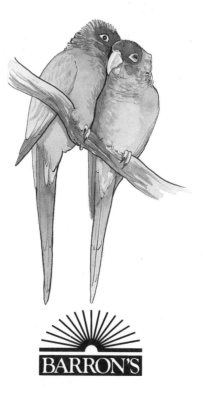

BARRON'S

Photo on Covers:
Front cover: Sun conure
Inside front cover: Golden headed (capped) conure
Inside back cover: Jenday conure
Back cover: Top left, Brewster's green conure (left) and Jenday conures (right); top right, dusky headed conure; bottom left, Patagonian conure; bottom right various *Aratinga* species.

All inquiries should be addressed to:
Barron's Educational Series, Inc.
250 Wireless Boulevard
Hauppauge, New York 11788

International Standard Book No. 0-8120-4880-6

Library of Congress Catalog Card No. 92-3941

Library of Congress Cataloging-in-Publication Data

Vriends, Matthew M., 1937-
    Conures : everything about purchase, housing, care, nutrition, breeding, and diseases, with a special chapter on understanding conures / Matthew M. Vriends : color photographs by outstanding animal photographers : drawings by Tanya M. Vriends and Michele Earle-Bridges.
        p. cm.
    Includes bibliographical references and index.
    ISBN 0-8120-4880-6
    1. Conures. I. Title.
SF473.C65V75   1992
636.6'865—dc20   92-3941
                                                                          CIP

PRINTED IN HONG KONG
21 20 19 18 17 16 15 14 13 12 11

About the Author:
Matthew M. Vriends is a Dutch-born biologist and ornithologist who holds a collection of advanced degrees, including a PhD in zoology. Dr. Vriends has written over 80 books in three languages on birds and other animals; his detailed works on parrotlike birds and finches are well known. Dr. Vriends has traveled extensively in South America, the United States, Africa, Australia, and Europe to observe and study birds in their natural environment and is widely regarded as an expert in tropical ornithology and aviculture. A source of particular pride are the many first-breeding results he has achieved in his large aviaries, which house more than 50 tropical bird species. Dr. Vriends and his family live near Cincinnati, Ohio. He is the author of three of Barron's Pet Owner's Manuals, *Lovebirds, Pigeons,* and *Gouldian Finches,* of Barron's Complete Nature Lover's Manual, *Feeding and Sheltering Backyard Birds,* and of four of Barron's Pet Owner's handbooks, *The New Bird Handbook, The New Cockatiel Handbook, The New Australian Parakeet Handbook,* and *The New Canary Handbook.*

Photo Credits:
Andy Cohen: page 63, top; back cover, top left. G. Ebben: page 9, bottom right; page 28, top right, bottom left; page 46, bottom; page 64; back cover, bottom. F. Mertens: page 27, top right; page 28, top left; page 45; page 46, top; page 63, bottom left. B. Everett Webb: front cover; inside front cover; page 9, top, bottom left; page 10; page 27, top left, bottom; page 28, bottom right; page 46, top; page 63, bottom right; inside back cover; back cover, top right.

Important Note:
The subject of this book is how to take care of Conures in captivity. In dealing with birds, always remember that newly purchased birds—even when they appear perfectly healthy—may be carriers of salmonellae. Therefore, it is highly advisable to have sample droppings analyzed by an avian veterinarian and to observe strict hygienic rules. Other infectious diseases that can endanger humans, such as ornithosis and tuberculosis, are rare in pet birds. Still, if you see a doctor because you or a member of your household has symptoms of a cold or the flu, mention that you keep birds. No one who is allergic to feathers or feather dust should keep birds.
    Most food insects are pests that can infest stored food and create a serious nuisance in your household. If you decide to grow any of these insects, be extremely careful to prevent them from escaping from their containers.

Contents

Preface

In this manual, you will find a detailed description of some of the more popular conures. Many of these birds can be procured in the pet trade.

Market channels for these birds are changing, however. Increasingly, their countries of origin are realizing the economic potential of their wildlife. Deforestation, however, is rapidly destroying wildlife habitats. According to the Pet Industry Joint Advisory Council (PIJAC), "Documentary evidence supports rates of deforestation between 50 and 75 acres per minute and upwards of 50,000 square miles per year because of agricultural and industrial expansion. Countries primarily affected are in the so-called Third World/underdeveloped areas such as Brazil (20 percent of rain forest destroyed by commercial cutting and mining); Indonesia (66 million acres classified as "denuded' by uncontrolled commercial cutting); Africa (1 million square kilometers of forest have been eliminated); Mexico (deforestation rate at 40,000 hectares per year); and Central America (almost two-thirds of Central America's lowland and lower mountain rain forest have been cleared or severely degraded since 1950)."

It is frightening to know that "…the world's rain forest will disappear altogether in 85 years if the present rate of 43,000 square miles per year continues," according to the Animal Welfare Institute.

Years ago, as a high school student, I became serious about raising "simple" tropical birds (finches, lovebirds, conures). Many people who noticed how I went about it called me a fanatic, or worse. Why should I be so intent about feeding, housing, nest boxes, temperature, and humidity on behalf of birds that could be replaced at any pet store for a couple of dollars? They thought it even stranger when they found out that I had made detailed observations about my breeding efforts and published the results in various bird journals.

Today, the average bird fancier as well as the bird expert have clearly come to a different conclusion. Every right-minded bird fancier tries to expand our pet bird stock, so that domestic breeding has completely (or almost completely) eliminated our dependence on imports. Many pet bird species, including some conures, have been domesticated, and imports of these species are no longer necessary. It is time to roll up our sleeves and develop effective programs to propagate other species in cages and aviary. The time will come when the breeding stock needed for such propagation will no longer be available because the birds may no longer be imported. It is—I hope—not too late!

I take great pride in those experiments that I conducted years ago—strange as my activities were regarded then. Let us work together to prevent the depredation of the rain forest, so that it will remain dynamic in our time and that of our descendants.

I hope this book will contribute to this effort.

I wish to thank J. Peter Hill, DVM, and Arthur Freud, publisher of *American Cage Bird Magazine,* for taking time from their busy schedules to review the manuscript and for the valuable contributions they have made to the text. My heartfelt thanks go also to my friend, the biologist and ornithologist John Coborn of Queensland, Australia, for the work he has taken off my hands. My wife, Lucia Vriends-Parent, I thank for her moral support and her editorial and ornithological expertise, my daughter Tanya, and good friends Michele Earle-Bridges and, last but not least, Don Reis and the dedicated staff at Barron's for their constant encouragement, enthusiasm, and spontaneous cooperation in the preparation of this work.

Readers' comments or suggestions to improve the text or expand it will be gratefully received, and I will consider using them for any later printing of this book.

Loveland, Ohio　　　　　　Matthew M. Vriends
Winter, 1991

Soyons fidèles à nos faiblesses
For Lucia, Tanya and Kimberley,
and Don Reis, friend and editor par excellence

Acquisition of Stock

The main aim of aviculturists is (or should be) the optimum welfare and breeding of the birds in their care—especially of species that are vulnerable. Indeed, some conures have already been declared endangered and are thus protected in the wild. Imported specimens of these species are no longer legally available. It is, therefore, the duty of every fancier to breed those species that are still available. Unfortunately, this is still not done sufficiently. If specimens are to be available in the future, they must be bred in sufficient quantities to preclude the need for further collection from the wild.

Various conure species are popular as house pets. Each year, many hundreds of these birds are hand-reared with this goal in mind. This, of course, is quite a different aspect of the bird fancy and one that (I think) has nothing or little to do with aviculture.

Nevertheless, whatever the situation and whatever birds you are interested in, you must see that you get the best stock possible. The best place to obtain birds is from a breeder who has a good name and reputation. Many such breeders now work closely with pet shops and supply them with good stock. The most important things to insist on are:
• The birds must be leg banded.
• They must be examined by a qualified avian veterinarian.

Since many veterinarians include an endoscopic examination (sexing of the bird by viewing the internal organs), the prospective purchaser may also receive a statement regarding the sex of the bird.

You must ask yourself the necessary questions before buying conures (or other animals for that matter). Since conures breed most readily in aviaries, you must have the necessary room in the garden or elsewhere. And, since conures are not particularly quiet, it would be a good idea to discuss your plans with your neighbors (although I must say that over the years, most conures become considerably quieter).

If you really want a tame house pet that is not too loud, you would be better off with an African gray parrot or one of the various Australian parrots. Nevertheless, you will find in the species descriptions (page 47 to page 77) which types are best suited to be kept as household pets without too many difficulties.

Be very sensible in your acquisition of birds. Shop around for quality and price! One of the most popular conures is the Queen of Bavaria conure, or golden conure *(Aratinga guarouba)*, from northeastern Brazil. This species is easy to tame and train, is talkative, comical, and affectionate. But take heed: it has a loud screech that can put the teeth of even the most ardent bird lover on edge! This species is very expensive and—alas—I have noticed that it is often bought for prestige rather than love. This, of course, is wrong. If you want to have such a bird but cannot afford the price, consider something else. The Jenday, or yellow-headed conure *(Aratinga auricapilla jandaya),* for example, is also attractive, comical, talkative, and affectionate, but much less expensive. In short, you must ask yourself why you need a particular species—for love, perhaps; certainly not for prestige; and, hopefully, with some thought for conservation.

Unfortunately, not all available birds are bred domestically. Many come from their native countries or from neighboring countries in order to circumvent strict export laws.* They may come from Europe, where bird breeding has had a high profile for centuries. Wherever they come from, however, most birds are wing-clipped before being placed in quarantine. After the four-week compulsory quarantine, the plumage can appear to have suffered considerable wear and tear, but with optimum care and feeding, the next molt will put things right. In order to buy a good, healthy bird, it is thus important to obtain one that looks healthy, has a

---

* However, a bill restricting bird importation may be enacted soon. Two such bills are currently (December 1991) being considered by Congress, and may be close to passage.

veterinary certificate, and is fully molted. If, after the molt (which takes place at least once per year), the plumage still leaves much to be desired, then it is perhaps best to forgo the purchase. Bald patches on the bird are a sign of self feather plucking. Such birds should not be purchased, as the habit is very difficult to cure.

Selecting Healthy Birds

Although wild conures are generally healthy, capture, transport, acclimatization and the quarantine period all reduce the birds' resistance to disease and put them in a stressful situation. A sick bird is usually recognized by the dullness of its plumage, which may also be ruffled and soiled. It will be lean and lethargic, and may have an eye or respiratory infection. It will sit cooped up in a corner looking very sorry for itself.

Healthy birds have a sleek, tight-fitting plumage, which insulates them from the cold and keeps up their resistance. One of the best means of detecting sick birds is to look at how they rest. Do not stick your nose up against the cage wire, as this will only alarm the birds and put them on alert. Stand back and observe them. If a bird rests on one foot, you can be almost certain that it is healthy. If it sleeps with two feet on the perch, then it is less likely to be healthy and you should not buy it.

Look also for bleeding feet—or worse—bleeding areas around the beak or on the body. Many conures under stress (particularly recently captured birds) suffer from vitamin K deficiency (conure bleeding syndrome or CBS). Vitamin K is required to synthesize the blood-clotting agent prothrombin. It is thus important that imported birds are given a good diet containing fruit, leafy green vegetables and tomatoes, and (in the breeding season) also a good commercial egg food. With a good diet, vitamin K is produced in the intestine by bacteria.

Healthy birds have firm droppings, which are coiled and formed around a whitish urine center;

the color is green to black, depending on the type of food and amount of water consumed (lots of fruit and vegetables cause a looser, greener stool). Most conures are susceptible to intestinal disorders, so keep an eye open! In such cases, warmth can be most helpful (see page 25).

Once you find a bird you may wish to purchase, ask the owner to take the bird in his or her hand. If you do this yourself, wear a heavy glove or wrap a towel around your hand, as even the smaller species can give a very powerful bite! Examining the bird carefully, go over the following points:
• The beak should close properly and be smooth in texture.
• Be sure there are no damaged wing feathers and that the tail is not soiled.
• Look at the feet one at a time; they should be clean and smooth.
• Palpate the flesh on either side of the breastbone; it should feel plump and firm, not hollow, with the breastbone protruding like a blade.
• Look at the area around the vent. If it is dirty and matted with droppings or stains, the bird may be suffering from some kind of intestinal disorder. For obvious reasons, such birds should not be purchased.
• Hold the bird to your ear (but keep clear of its beak!) and listen to its breathing. If you hear a squeaking or rasping noise, the bird probably has a respiratory infection and should not be purchased.
• Beware of birds that sit on their perch bobbing their head and moving their tail back and forth; this is almost always due to breathing difficulties, and probably indicates a respiratory problem.
• Blow open the feathers on the breast. The skin you can see should look clean and healthy, not spotty or red.

If the above criteria are met, you can be pretty sure of getting a healthy specimen. Make sure you know what the bird has been getting to eat. Diets should be changed gradually over a period of 10 to 14 days.

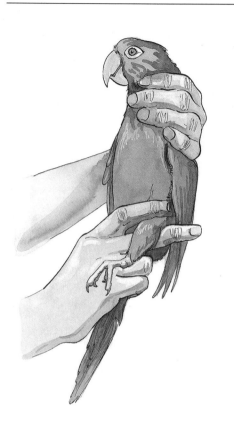

Restraining a conure. Never grip tightly and don't press hard on the neck; this could compress the upper end of the bird's trachea or windpipe.

Always pick up birds yourself. Do not allow them to be delivered by train or plane unless you have a trusted colleague who can inspect them first. Always ask for guarantees and take as few risks as possible.

Note: If you are planning to breed conures, do not rely on visual clues to select a true pair. Most conure species are difficult to distinguish between the sexes. The only certain way is to have them endoscopically examined by a veterinarian (see page 35). The age and sexual maturity are also difficult to determine. I believe smaller species are ready for breeding when they are two years old; medium to large species are ready when three-and-a-half to four years old.

Acclimatization

Newly imported birds are not acclimatized. They are not accustomed to the cage or aviary, although the official quarantine will have got them used to a certain amount of confinement. It is therefore recommended that new birds be placed in a cage (preferably one bird per cage). These birds are quite wild and nervous and, in an aviary, could fly into the wire and kill themselves. In order to reduce casualties during transport and acclimatization, newly imported birds are often wing clipped. There is no point in placing such birds in an aviary!

Find out what the birds are eating. It will probably not be a diet "by the book," so it will have to be improved—but *gradually*, over a period of at least 14 days.

The new birds will want peace and quiet. Disturb them as little as possible, and only one person should care for them during the first week. Do not stand in front of the wire for too long; the birds will flutter around wildly, and there is a danger they may injure themselves.

After three weeks the new birds should be paired and placed in larger cages until their wing feathers have fully grown again.

Housing, Care, and Management

The Cage

In general, conures are lively birds but there are also some, especially the *Brotogeris* species, that spend hours—sometimes a whole day and night—sitting in their sleeping box. Experience has shown that each pair of birds is best housed in its own aviary and that the birds are most likely to breed in such a situation. Conures can also be kept in cages, the best being the so-called breeding cages, which are totally enclosed except for the wire front. Such a cage can never be too large. Minimum measurements for the smaller species are 24 inches long, 16 inches wide and 20 inches high (60 x 40 x 50 cm). Larger species should have a minimum size of 44 x 26 x 40 inches (120 x 65 x

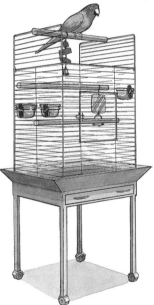

An all-wire cage. Note the many extras: casters for easy reposition, a roomy metal base to avoid spilling of seed hulls and bedding, an all-metal tray, various metal containers for food and water, a wide door that can be used as a platform for easy "landing" and entering the cage, and a roof that can be opened and made into a play area.

100 cm). All cage birds should also have the opportunity of exercising for a couple of hours daily in the room (beware of damage to furniture, etc. from the sharp beaks of the conures!).

Cages should never be round, but square or rectangular with horizontal wires, so that the birds can climb. In order to facilitate cleaning, a sliding floor tray should be installed; store-bought cages usually have this feature. Cover the floor of the cage with a thick layer of corncob or other absorbent material.

Perches supplied with cages are often too thin. Ensure that perches are about ¾ to 1 inch (2–2.5 cm) in diameter, so that the birds' claws cannot quite reach around them; the birds will then have a better grip, and their toenails are less likely to become overgrown. Natural perches are extremely useful (for example, twigs from willow, poplar, or fruit trees). These are not only gnawed at (providing good exercise for the beak, relief from boredom, and a valuable additive to the diet), but the varying thicknesses of the branches provide excellent exercise for the muscles of the feet and help abrade the toenails to a suitable length. Other occupational "toys" also help relieve boredom. Bird owners can take advantage of the development and availability of toys that have been designed with safety and the bird's activity in mind. These are generally made with untreated leather and wood from trees that pose no chemical threats to birds. Some of the more inventive toys have had the leather and wood brightened with food coloring (see page 12).

Top left: The sharp-tailed conure (*Aratinga a. acuticaudata*) is one of the more magnificent of all Aratingas. Trained properly, these birds become affectionate pets.
Top right: Finsch's conure (*A. (holochlora) finschi*) has yellow-colored small underwing feathers—which none of the other "holochora" species has.
Bottom left: Famous bird park Loro Parque in Tenerife, Spain, bred the mitered conure (*A. m. mitrata*) in 1981.
Bottom right: The red-masked conure (*A. erythrogenys*) has the most red on the head of all the Aratinga species.

Housing, Care, and Management

Ensure that the drink and feeding hoppers are not too small. I give the birds separate dishes from which they can easily extract the seeds they require at that particular moment.

Some American aviculturists regularly achieve good breeding results in surprisingly small cages (48 x 16 x 16 inches; 120 x 40 x 40 cm). However, I recommend that in such small cages the sleeping and/or nesting boxes are affixed *outside* the cage, so that the space in the cage is not further reduced. Access to these boxes is by means of a hole at the end or back of the cage. Personal experience has shown me that conures do best in *very large* cages or aviaries, where their lively and active character is repressed as little as possible. When kept in too small accommodations, such birds can become depressed or develop unpleasant habits (such as plucking out their feathers or those of their partners).

Perches

Perches must be placed in front of the seed trays, cups, and water containers. At least one perch should be placed high in the cage, since conures (like all other birds) love roosting as high as possible.

Do not fill the cage with too many perches. There should be plenty of space for the birds to move about. Moreover, do not place the perches directly above each other; otherwise the droppings of the upper bird will soil the plumage of the lower. *Never* cover perches with sandpaper sleeves. As R. Dean Axelson, DVM, says: "Making a bird stand on a sandpaper-covered perch is comparable to making someone walk along a gravel road in bare feet."

◄ Top: The golden-headed or capped conure (*Aratinga a. auricapilla*), a rare bird in the wild, is bred regularly in captivity. Bottom: The jenday conure (*A. auricapillus jandaya*) is hardy and a good breeder. It needs a strongly constructed, roomy nest box as it will rapidly destroy exposed woodwork.

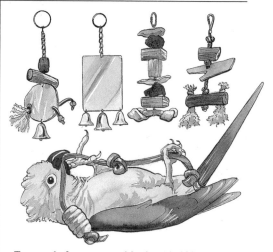

Toys made from untreated leather (rawhide) and wood from trees that pose no chemical threats to birds. Be sure that the links of the chains are large enough to prevent accidents, such as catching the bird's toes. Mirrors and other shiny objects must be "unbreakable."

Perches should not all be equally thick; variations in thickness will offer relaxation to muscles of the leg and foot. Put elder, willow, eucalyptus, and small fruit tree branches in the cage, particularly branches with bark on them. Do not use tree branches that have been sprayed with insecticides.

Mirrors

Conures, especially those housed alone, love to play with mirrors and observe themselves from all sides. Use very strong, securely framed mirrors that cannot be gnawed through; avoid using those made of glass, and purchase only the new plexiglass mirrors. They are almost as reflective as glass and are virtually impossible to break. Mirrors should be part of every cage.

When the birds are allowed to fly about in the room, be careful with any mirrors, as these will invariably be inspected. When the birds are let free in the room for the first time, cover all mirrors with a piece of cloth (and, for that matter, any window

11

as well). After a few days, when the birds have become accustomed to the room, you may remove the cloth.

There is one disadvantage in giving mirrors to conures. Sometimes birds become so taken with their own reflection that they no longer have an eye for their partner. I feel we should take this risk when the conure is alone too much. If, after some time, it appears that the bird is growing too interested in its own reflection, remove the mirror and replace it with some other toys. You should then pay extra attention to your little friend to alleviate the loss of its "partner."

The Cage Bottom

Every well-constructed cage has a pull-out bottom tray to facilitate cleaning. Certain tub cages can be completely removed from their bottom. Cover the drawer with a strong piece of brown paper or wrapping paper, and strew a ¾-inch (2-cm) layer of shell sand or corncob on top. Remember, however, that ground corncob, because it is made of organic matter, can encourage bacterial growth. This is actually true, not only of corncob, but also of paper and any other bedding material you might use. If cages are maintained as noted below, the growth of bacteria will not be a problem. Avoid newspaper, as the birds will gnaw on it and ingest harmful substances from the ink.

To avoid or reduce spilling sand or corncob, attach glass or a clear plastic strip about 4 inches (10 cm) high around the cage. Usually, this is standard equipment, but ornamental cages are often sold without it, and you must install the strip or guard yourself.

Clean the cage bottom at least once a week, which means replacing the paper and "bedding."

Toys

Conures often amuse themselves with all kinds of playthings; in this respect they resemble lovebirds and budgerigars (parakeets). Every bird store

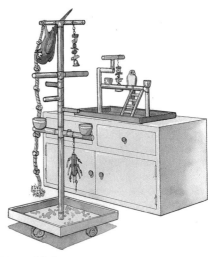

Two useful play pens.

or pet shop offers ample choices, so you can make your bird happy quickly and simply.

Too many toys in the cage will not present a tidy sight, and the birds may become more interested in these knickknacks than in you! This is a distraction to taming your conures. In addition, too many toys take up space that the bird needs for climbing and wing flapping activities. Personally, I prefer playgrounds outside the cage, usually a square tray made of sheet metal, plastic, or wood, on which various wooden toys can be placed.

When the bird is allowed outside the cage, a platform on the threshold seems useful, if not necessary. It makes it considerably easier for birds to enter the cage. This "runway" is best constructed of wood and is easy to move. New runways may have to be made regularly, which shouldn't be too much effort, even for a person who is not especially handy.

Covering the Cage

Conures need to have 10 to 12 hours of rest each day. Therefore, do not expose your birds to too much noise. If you have a television in the same room as the cage, shield the cage with a cloth at the appropriate times. Although it may be impossible for people to detect the rapid changes of dot patterns on the color TV screen, most birds see this, and it is bad for their eyes. The farther away the cage is placed from the TV, the less damage will be inflicted. Studies have shown that it is best to shield the cage when the distance between the cage and set is less than 16 feet (5 m).

Many bird fanciers maintain that a cage should be completely covered with some kind of cloth during the evening and at night. However, not every conure is thrilled with this arrangement. I believe that the best method is to cover just one side and/or the top of the cage so that no direct light or TV emissions shine on the bird. Thus the bird may decide for itself whether or not to sit in the light.

Safety Precautions

When you allow your conure to fly about the home for a few hours, be sure that all windows and doors are firmly closed, that the drapes have been drawn—or you can place decals, not only to alert the birds, but also for the safety of humans who may also mistake the large glass door for an opening—that the fireplace has been safely covered by a screen, and that all electrical appliances and stoves have been switched off. Any fans in use on hot days should also be switched off or covered with screening, so that the birds cannot get at them.

Indoor plants and flowers may also cause problems. Conures are very curious and are bound to inspect your plants sooner or later. Since various plants are poisonous (see table on this page), it is well to keep vigilant. Plants such as cacti can cause serious injuries. Therefore, it is best to remove all plants from the room or to cover them temporarily with plastic.

Special Summer Care

Scrupulous cleanliness is essential to bird keeping. As temperatures rise, most soft foods (egg

Some of the More Common Potentially Poisonous House Plants	
Amaryllis	(*Amaryllis* species)
Autumn Crocus	(*Colchicum* species)
Azalea	(*Azalea* species)
Balsam Pear	(*Memordica charantia*)
Bird of Paradise	(*Poinciana gilliensii*)
Boxwood	(*Buxus* species)
Caladium	(*Caladium* species)
Castor Bean	(*Ricinus communis*)
Chalice Vine	(*Solandra* species)
Coral Plant	(*Jatropha multifida*)
Daffodil	(*Narcissus* species)
Datura (berries only)	(*Datura* species)
Dieffenbachia	(*Dieffenbachia picta*)
Elephant's Ear	(*Colocasia* species)
Hyacinth	(*Galtonia* species)
Hydrangea	(*Hydrangea macrophylla*)
Japanese Yew	(*Taxus cuspidata*)
Java Beans	(*Phaseolus lunatus* var.)
Lantana	(*Lantana* species)
Lily-of-the-Valley	(*Convallaria majalis*)
Narcissus	(*Narcissus* species)
Nightshade (Deadly, Black, Garden or Woody Nightshade, and Eggplant [all except fruit])	(Solanaceae)
Oleander	(*Nerium* species)
Philodendron	(*Philodendron* species)
Rhododendron	(*Rhododendron* species)
Yam Bean	(*Pachyrhisus erosus*)

food, universal food, milk-soaked bread, green food, or fruit) will turn bad very quickly. Higher temperatures enable many harmful organisms to multiply rapidly. Therefore, inspect the cage, preferably every day, and observe extreme cleanliness.

Birds living indoors for the greater part of the year should be taken outside at intervals—the more the better—during the spring and summer months. Do not place the cage in full sunshine but in a shady environment out of reach of cats, dogs, and other predators. If you own cats, constant vigilance is vital. Many a cat has made victims of a fancier's birds, and if you are not careful your bird may meet this fate. Place the cage (without the metal or plastic bottom) on the grass, where the birds may walk about at will. In the afternoon you may hose down the grass, providing it is a warm summer day.

Bathing

Many conures delight in rolling about in moist (insecticide-free!) grass, especially in the morning when the grass is still covered with dew. This is an unforgettable sight for the fancier. Or you can achieve a comparable effect by placing freshly washed greens, such as the leaves and stems of carrots, beets and similar vegetables, on top of their cage. They will pull these greens in and get their shower at the same time they are ingesting a nutritious treat. This "bath in the morning" cannot always be provided in captivity, though much can be achieved in an aviary.

Bird shops sell small plastic or metal bathing "tubs," which are actually intended for canaries and tropical and subtropical cage birds. These can be hung over the cage threshold in the morning or, if desired, throughout the day. These bathing tubs are far too small for the larger conure species, and not all dwarf conures will make use of them either.

Conures will often take a "shower" at the water tray by quickly ducking their heads in the water. Wet grass sod on the bottom of the cage or a few wet lettuce leaves in the bathing dishes are always welcome. Birds that are regularly allowed out of their cages will sooner or later discover your dripping kitchen faucet (and if it is not dripping, you can let it drip). When a bird has made a habit of taking a shower under the kitchen faucet, make sure that the hot water tap is firmly turned off. You may also find that, for some reason, your birds will bathe in their water dishes when the room in which they live is vacuumed. Many people have reported this behavior, and the best explanation that we have is that the birds relate the sound of the vacuum to a

A Nanday conure taking a shower under the kitchen faucet.

rainstorm or rushing water and are thus stimulated to bathe.

If the birds dislike bathing, you must wash them yourself from time to time. Before an exhibition you will have to bathe your birds at least a week before the show, preferably earlier. We only bathe birds when it is absolutely necessary.

Since a bird's body is very fragile, be exceptionally careful about handling and holding it. Before taking the bird from its cage, prepare two shallow bowls or plates with warm water, about 80° F (26° C), in which some soft soap has been dissolved. A good brand of dish detergent may also be used for this purpose. Hold the bird in such a way that you can support its head with your thumb and forefinger. Then immerse it carefully in the bowl with the dissolved soap, in such a way that its head is not brought in contact with the water (in order to prevent soap from coming into its eyes, nose, and bill).

When you have immersed the animal several times, take an old shaving brush with soft bristles

14

(which you wet first in the saucer with soap) and stroke the feathers in the direction of the tail. Do not forget the area around the anus (vent). You can clean the head and neck with a soft, natural sponge. Make certain not to rub soap into the bill, nose, or eyes of the conure. To give the wings a good wash, spread them across the edge of the plate. You can do the same with the tail, but do this carefully to avoid accidental feather loss, which is ruinous for show birds.

The bowl with clean water is used to rinse the bird. Immerse the bird a few times in the water, and restore its shape with a clean brush.

Finally the bird must be dried, which is best performed by using a thick towel that has been warmed a little.

After bathing and drying, place the bird in a clean, not-too-large cage without bedding, in a warm room. Never put the bird outside in the sun or too close to a stove. Do not remove the bird from this room until the following day (to prevent it from catching a cold). Make sure the room is not too hot either, otherwise the feathers will curl. A hair dryer may be helpful, but remain in the immediate vicinity to prevent accidents.

The Aviary

A garden aviary in which each breeding pair of birds has its own flight and night shelter is ideal. Since most conure species are born "carpenters," it is best to have as little exposed woodwork as possible inside the aviary. In fact, metal framing is best for these birds. Metal lasts longer, does not provide a home for parasites, does not get eaten by termites, and is not affected by dry or wet rot. If galvanized, the metal will not rust and should last a lifetime.

Acclimation to the Temperate Zone

Once acclimated (see page 7), tropical conures are surprisingly hardy in our temperate climates,

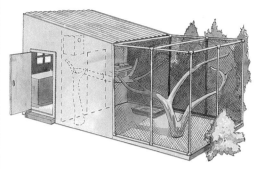

A two-part garden aviary.

but they still need some form of protection from our cold winds, driving rain, and harsh frosts. The aviary should therefore have a night shelter, which can be closed off in inclement weather and heated if necessary, especially in the late fall and winter. Conures will gladly seek the warmth and shelter when the weather outside gets unpleasant. To keep out cold and damp, the pophole through which the birds enter and leave the shelter should be as small as possible. It can be fitted with a sliding door operated by a chain or rod from outside the aviary, so that you can lock birds in (or out) as necessary.

Heating used in the shelter should be minimal. Usually, all that is required is a simple 100-watt light bulb (colored red or blue to minimize disturbance at night) to eliminate freezing temperatures. Greater heating is dangerous, since the temperature difference between the inside and outside will be too great—a sure way of reducing a bird's resistance to disease or causing other upsets to the metabolism.

Be careful at all times when transferring a bird from an indoor cage or aviary to an outdoor aviary. In summer (after May) this can usually be done without too many problems. After August it can become quite risky, since the bird is not yet accustomed to the outdoor fluctuations in temperatures. If you receive recently imported birds (after the official quarantine period) late in the year, then (depending on where you live) it is usually advisable to house them indoors where you can maintain them at a minimum of 64° F (18° C). You will then be able to acclimatize them to an outdoor aviary the following summer.

Sleeping boxes (which will be later used as nesting boxes) can also be hung up in the night shelter. These must be made from strong, hardwood as the birds will soon start trying to carve them up. The edges of the box and the entrance hole can be protected with sheet (galvanized) steel or aluminium. Conures will often attempt to "eat through" the sleeping/nestbox from the inside out and may completely destroy it unless it is carefully constructed.

Landscaping

Planting trees or shrubs *inside* an aviary is a complete waste of time. These would be demolished by the birds in no time at all. However, an old tree trunk (willow, for example) placed in the aviary will be enjoyed enormously by the birds!

In the wild most conures inhabit woodland border areas. It is therefore recommended that the area around the aviary be planted with trees and shrubs to give the birds a feeling of protection. This will increase their chances of breeding successfully. Ensure that no poisonous plants are used near the aviary and that shrubs or creepers do not damage the aviary wire. Regular pruning may be necessary. Also, do not plant so thickly that you cannot see the birds or that the sun is completely excluded from the flight. With a little forethought and artistic acumen, you can create an area of aesthetic beauty and attraction.

Stocking

Keeping more than one species together is not recommended. The few times that I have placed (of necessity) pairs of different species together in an aviary have ended in disaster. Even closely related birds or those of the same species will sooner or later enter into serious squabbling.

Some of the More Common Potentially Poisonous Outdoor Plants

American Yew	(*Taxus canadensis*)
Baneberry	(*Actaea* species)
Bittersweet Nightshade	(*Solanum dulcamara*)
Black Locust	(*Robinia pseudoacacia*)
Bloodroot	(*Sanguinario* species)
Buckthorn	(*Rhamnus* species)
Buttercup	(*Ranunculus* species)
Calla Lily	(*Zantedeschia aethiopica*)
Cherry Tree	(*Prunus* species)
Christmas Candle	(*Pedilanthus tithymaloides*)
Clematis	(*Clematis* species)
Cowslip	(*Caltha* species)
Daphne	(*Daphne* species)
English Holly	(*Ilex aquifolium*). For aviaries with parrotlike birds, thrushes, etc.
English Yew	(*Taxus baccata*)
Golden Chain or Laburnum	(*Laburnum anagyroides*)
Henbane	(*Hyoscyamus niger*)
Hemlock	(*Conium maculatum*)
Honey Locust	(*Gleditsia triacathos*)
Horse Chestnut	(*Aesculus* species)
Indian Turnip	(*Arisaema triphyllum*)
Iris	(*Iris* species)
Jimsonweed	(*Datura* species)
Larkspur	(*Delphinium* species)
Locoweed	(*Astragalus mollissimus*)
Lords and Ladies	(*Arum* species)
May Apple	(*Podophyllum* species)
Mistletoe (only the berries)	(*Santalales* species)
Monkshood	(*Aconitum* species)
Morning Glory	(*Ipomoea* species)
Mountain Laurel	(*Kalmia latifolia*)
Nutmeg	(*Myristica fragrans*)
Pokeweed	(*Phytolacca amaricana*)
Rhubarb	(*Rheum rhaponticum*)
Rosary Peas	(*Abrus precatorius*)
Snowdrop	(*Galanthus nivalis*)
Snowflake	(*Leucoium vernum*)
Sweet Pea	(*Lathyrus latifolius*)
Tobacco	(*Nicotiana* species)
Water Hemlock	(*Cicuta maculata*)
Western Yew	(*Taxus breviflora*)

Housing, Care, and Management

I once experimented with a 33-foot (10-m) flight with four separate night shelters. A pair of birds was left in each of the shelters (thus four pairs of birds) for two weeks before being allowed access to the flight. In this way, the birds in the flight could just about stand each other, and, in the case of minor skirmishes, the vanquished could quickly find solace in its own shelter. This was all right until the victor decided to follow the vanquished into its shelter and lay claim to that as well! Eventually, I had to step in and mediate. Since then I have not attempted similar experiments!

Thus it is best to keep conures together in single pairs only. This system also ensures better control with regard to sickness.

Construction

Keep the shape of your aviary straight and simple. The birds should be the focus of your attention, not the domes, steeples, and towers sometimes seen. Try to have the aviary's shape conform to the surroundings. If you have no location that already meets these requirements, you will have to make the adjustments yourself by attractive, natural planting.

Although a natural earth floor has many advantages, a cement or concrete floor is the better choice if you wish to keep and breed conures. A concrete floor can be hosed off daily, ridding it of any droppings (worm infection!) and other dirt the birds have made. Part of the floor could be planted with sod; many birds enjoy frolicking on grass moist with dew or under the gentle spray of a garden hose. If you find it impossible to keep the sod alive, place it in low wooden boxes that can be removed whenever you wish to check or replace them without upsetting the birds.

The covered portion of the aviary run should have a watertight roof (preferably of sheet-corrugated fiberglass or sturdy plastic to transmit light), a back wall made of planking or concrete bricks (although fiberglass would do just as well), and the rest made of wire mesh. A removable dividing wall can be built to separate the open area from the covered part of the flight. You might wish to put this divider (also made of mesh) into place during extended periods of bad weather. Some bird fanciers use mesh for the wall of the night shelter that adjoins the flight. I am not in favor of this, because I feel it does not afford enough protection against the elements. It also means you cannot provide heat in the night shelter, should this ever be desirable; with one wall made of mesh, that would be senseless.

The floor of the covered section should also be of concrete. A floor constructed of cement tiles is also perfectly acceptable. Such a floor, however, should be generously covered with coarse sand, in which the conures enjoy picking and sand bathing. The "natural growth" in this setting would consist of one or more dead trees, supplemented with artificial perches and tree twigs in pots and tubs.

The sides and roof of the night shelter can be built using vertical tongue-and-groove boards. All windows, doors, etc. should be properly hung and should close tightly. To avoid puddles (and the consequent rotting of materials), make sure the roof is built on a slant and extends on all sides. It should be completely waterproof.

The final touches consist of thoroughly staining all parts of the aviary. In fact, to help prevent warping of the wood, you should treat all the wood with stain before you begin the aviary. All wooden edges should be protected with metal strips. The wire should be given a coat of stain (use an almost dry brush), which also helps to make the birds more visible. The night shelter should not be painted. If you wish to paint the inside, use child-safe paints (used for children's furniture), since these paints do not contain any harmful ingredients (e.g., lead).

The ideal length of the aviary flight should be ten times the length of the bird. Thus if a species is 10 inches (25 cm) long, then the flight (less night shelter) should be 10 x 10 inches = 100 inches (8.3 feet), or 4 m. If the bird is 12 inches (30 cm) long, then the length is 10 x 12 inches = 120 inches (10 feet), or 4.73 m. The width and the height of the flight should always be 6 feet (2 m); the height of the night shelter should be 6 feet and 15¾ inches (2.4 m). Birds always tend to find the highest spot to roost at night; by having the highest perches in the night shelter, they are more likely to sleep under cover—especially important during the colder parts of the year.

Perches

A selection of perches of varying thickness should be available both in the flight and the shelter. Roosting perches in particular should not be too thin, otherwise the bird's toes will not be protected by the plumage and may be exposed to cold and frost. Natural perches will have to be changed more frequently than artificial ones, but the latter provide your birds with little amusement.

Since conures are quite active, you needn't cram the aviary with perches. Those supplied should be placed in strategic positions, leaving adequate, uncluttered flying spaces for the birds. In the shelter you can place a 10-inch-wide (25 cm) plank about 20 inches (50 cm) below the ceiling as well as a few perches along the walls. The plank will be used by the conures for resting and sleeping.

Perches in the aviary, like those used in cages, should be made of hardwood. Provide your birds with twigs and small branches from willow and fruit trees (apple and pear, *not* cherry), so that they can gnaw these rather than the perches. Another advantage of providing twigs for gnawing is that your birds won't start the bad habit of pecking at each other's feathers. Affix the perches at both ends of the flight so that they do not interfere with the length of the flight available to the birds. Perches should not be installed too close to the wire, however, because of cats, which can pose a definite danger, and because the birds' tail feathers will eventually become frayed if they are constantly rubbed against the wire. If you can place an old tree trunk in the center of the aviary or build the aviary around one, by all means do so!

Bathing Facilities

Every aviary should be equipped with flat ceramic saucers allowing the birds to bathe. On colder days these dishes should be removed. Make sure that your birds are dry before they go to sleep; that is, they should not bathe after 4 or 5 P.M. You could also put a garden sprinkler to good use; many birds prefer a gentle shower to a tub bath. Perches should not be situated above any of these bathing or drinking facilities. The water in the saucers should be changed daily.

Water and Seed Dishes

Use indestructible seed feeders that are easily cleaned and made so that the conures cannot soil the contents and sit or walk on the seeds. Wooden feeders would soon be reduced to splinters. There are several feeders on the market, and local pet shop staff can advise you about them. Saucers made of glass, ceramic, or similar material can be used for both seeds and water. Automated watering systems are also available and, although these are more expensive than water dishes, they do provide fresh water at all times for your bird.

The most practical feeders are the boxlike hoppers with glass fronts called self-feeders. These hoppers usually hold quantities of seeds sufficient for a number of days. They are often divided into narrow compartments in which each type of seed can be given separately, enabling the birds to make their own mixture to suit their needs. At the bottom of these feeders there is a detachable tray designed to catch seeds thrown aside by the birds.

The Bird Room

The bird room is simply an outside aviary brought indoors. An attic, basement, or other available room in the house will make an admirable bird room. To construct the bird room you merely have to fit wire screens over the windows and build a little "porch," by means of an extra wire door, to prevent the birds from escaping. The rest of the setup is the same as for the outside aviary.

The bird room is used for breeding small conures. It is also suitable for keeping more exotic species, especially those that cannot tolerate temperate or cold climates very well. Very expensive species are often kept this way. Bird rooms are often used by more experienced fanciers, but the beginning bird enthusiast can also achieve successful breeding results in a bird room.

Always try to achieve a natural effect. Use tiles for the floor, and place a layer of clean sand on top, which must be refreshed regularly. On top of the sand place a layer of corncob or grass fiber cage bedding (a special blend of grass fibers in pelleted form). Twigs must be placed in tubs and pots.

With a little artistic insight and imagination, you can create a beautiful corner of Nature inside your own home!

The Indoor Aviary

An indoor aviary is a small aviary placed in a room or an attic, around which are grouped arrangements of plants. The setup is the same as in an outside aviary. Many people confuse an indoor aviary with a bird room. A bird room is an entire room set up only to house birds. The indoor aviary is placed in a room where other activities take place.

The indoor aviary is currently very popular; some manufacturers even provide ready-made models that meet the necessary requirements. I have seen some indoor aviaries that were truly beautiful and in which successful breeding results were achieved regularly. The birds seemed unconcerned by the children playing nearby on the floor.

Nest Boxes

Nest boxes should be made from hardwood (oak or beech, for example), since conures are very destructive and will soon decimate a softwood structure. Eggs or young have been known to fall out of a damaged nest box and perish on the aviary floor.

The interior of the nest box should be covered with strong mesh (take care not to leave any sharp ends that could injure adults or young). The floor of the box should be covered with a thick, upturned sod (sawdust, washed aquarium sand, or wood pulp can also be used). Mix a little damp earth with the floor covering to help prevent desiccation. Sawdust and wood pulp that are totally dry can cause asthmatic conditions or encourage aspergillosis. Do not be surprised if a hen throws everything out and prefers to lay her eggs on the bare floor.

A choice of various types of nest boxes is good. The same types should be placed both in and outside the shelter, giving the birds a wide variety of sites. Most likely the birds will choose a site inside the shelter, since they prefer dark or secluded spots. Always take note of the type of site and box preferred by a particular pair. You will then know what to offer in the next breeding season.

Do not be surprised if the birds pick out the smallest nest box you have offered.

An L-shaped conure nest box, as used by the author.

Feeding

In the wild many conures, including *Aratinga* species, live in damp or dry savanna regions, where the rainfall frequently is less than 39⅓ inches (1000 cm) per year. Others live in thorn bush savannas *(A. cactorum)* or in the mountains *(A. mistrata alticola)* at an altitude of 10,000 feet (3,000 m). The birds normally live in family groups, and scarce food supplies are soon used up. Many species travel great distances in search of food and water; once they find an adequate source, it is not unusual to find hundreds of birds reaping the benefits.

Most conures feed on ripe and unripe grass seeds, fruits (including cactus), berries, nuts, flowers, buds, insects, and grains (frequently to the great annoyance of farmers). Many conures have become so-called culture followers and are frequently seen in huge flocks on agricultural land.

A Good Diet

Most birds are not fed according to their physiological needs—and many are forced to eat foods to which they are not accustomed. Often, ignorance is to blame. Amateur bird keepers are apt to feed their feathered friends the wrong things or in the wrong amounts. Even bird fanciers can make incredible mistakes when feeding their pets.

A good diet is one that keeps a bird at an optimal standard of health. It also ensures a long, trouble-free life. A good diet should include the following chemical components:

- Proteins: nitrogenous organic compounds of high molecular weight that occurs in all living cells and that are required for all life processes in plants and animals.
- Carbohydrates: organic compounds composed of carbon, hydrogen, and oxygen, including sugars and starches.
- Fats: greasy substances composed of carbon, hydrogen, and oxygen that form the chief part of adipose tissue in animals and plants.

- Vitamins: organic substances essential in small quantities for normal metabolism and health; found in foods and also produced synthetically (see Tables on the following page).
- Minerals: inorganic substances occurring in nature, having a definite chemical composition and usually of definite crystal structure.
- Water.

A deficiency of one or more of these constituents will result in bodily malfunction. Some dietary constituents can be stored in the body and kept in reserve; others must be consumed daily. Birds suffering from dietary deficiencies become weak and lose their resistance to disease.

Food Requirements

A bird's food requirements are determined by its physiological condition, its activity level, and the demands of its habitat (cage or aviary). Growth, breeding, egg-laying, rearing young, molting—all increase a bird's food requirements.

Food provides the bird with energy, which is essential for a bird to be active and maintain its body temperature when environmental temperatures are low. When the bird's body temperature becomes too high or too low, its resistance is reduced and it becomes susceptible to all types of diseases.

An adult bird that is very active requires more energy, which must come from the diet. The number of hours of sunlight also influence the bird's behavior. When molting, birds lose relatively more body heat and require more energy. They also require larger amounts of proteins to replace feathers.

Breeding birds requires more fat in the diet as reserve energy. During brooding, when birds leave the nest infrequently, these reserve fats ensure a constant body temperature. To manufacture eggs, female conures require extra nutrients. At first these substances are drawn from current food

Feeding

Fat-Soluble Vitamins

Vitamin	Functions	Sources
A	Metabolism of body cells; maintenance of skin, bone, and mucous membranes; prevention of night blindness; synthesis of visual pigments.	Egg yolk; fresh leafy greens (chickweed, spinach, dandelion); yellow and orange vegetables and fruits; fish liver oils.
D_3	Promotes absorption of calcium and phosphorus; prevents egg binding; essential for blood clotting.	Fish liver oils and egg yolk; produced in skin that is exposed to ultraviolet light (sunlight).
E	Prevents oxidation of vitamin A and degeneration of fatty acids; important for development of brain cells, muscles, blood, sexual organs, and the embryo; increases blood circulation.	Wheat germ and corn germ oils, fruits and vegetables, chickweed, watercress, spinach and kale, germinated seeds.
K	Promotes blood clotting and liver functions.	Green food, carrot tops, kale, alfalfa, tomatoes, egg yolk, soy oil, and fish meal; synthesized by bacteria in the intestine.

Water-Soluble Vitamins

Vitamin	Functions	Sources
B_1 (Thiamine)	Assists in overall growth; metabolic functions; growth of muscles and nervous system.	Germ cells of grain seeds, legumes, yeast, fruits, egg, liver.
B_2 (Riboflavin)	Egg production; metabolic functions; proper development of skin, feathers, beak, and nails.	Yeast, eggs, green leaves, germ of good quality seeds.
B_3 (Niacin)	Production of hormones; metabolic functions; proper function of nervous and digestive systems.	Peanuts, corn, whole grains, liver, lean meats.
B_6 (Pyridoxine)	Assists in the production of digestive juices, red blood cell, and antibodies.	Bananas, peanuts, beans, whole grain cereals, egg yolk.
B_{12} (Cyanocobalamin)	Assists in the production of red blood cells; is essential for metabolism.	Fish meal, liver, eggs, insects, vitamin supplements (all plants are low in B_{12}).
Biotin	Assists in the metabolism of various acids and nucleic acid synthesis.	Egg yolk, nuts, greens.
C (Ascorbic Acid)	Assists in the metabolism of various acids, healing of wounds, tissue growth, and red blood cell formation; promotes absorption of iron.	Citrus fruits and juices, leafy greens, fresh fruits, cabbage.

reserves; in times of shortage they are drawn from the body tissues.

Conures must receive an adequate amount of vitamins and minerals. A deficiency of one or more of these will lead to diseases of one sort or another. This can lead to sterility in adult birds, inadequate fertilization, dead nestlings, and decreased resistance to infectious diseases. The calcium required to manufacture eggshells can weaken the mother's bones if she doesn't receive an adequate supply in the diet before and during the breeding season.

Conures are altricial birds (staying in the nest for some time while being cared for by the parents); they are born naked and take several days to develop down feathers. The quality of food these birds receive is very important for optimum growth and bone and feather development.

Food Choices

Habit plays an important role in a bird's choice of foods. Therefore, changes in a bird's diet should be made very gradually. Take care when changing over to rearing food or food concentrates. It is unrealistic to expect a parent bird to change to rearing food just a few days before its brood hatches.

Birds recognize food by its appearance, texture, and taste. If a bird receives pelleted food in place of a seed mixture, the size of the pellets will play a part in their acceptability. Birds prefer certain seeds over others because of the hardness or softness of the seed husks or their taste. The amount of sugar in the seed can also influence its acceptability.

Traditional Foods

Conures are not particularly fussy about their food. A good mixture of seeds, various fruits and green food, and some cuttlebone will keep them happy. A good variety of seeds is important. But beware of sunflower seeds; give them in only small quantities. Conures get to like sunflower seeds so

much that they will ignore other seeds. Since sunflower seed are deficient in lysine (an amino acid essential for plumage development), an "addicted" bird can have a very poor plumage, or no feathers at all! For small conures, such as most of the *Pyrrhura* species, sunflower seeds are very fattening. Keep the following rules:

• Small conures should never have more than 25 percent of sunflower seeds in their seed mixture.
• Large conures should never have more than 35 percent of sunflower seeds in their seed mixture.

Conures must also have starchy (high-carbohydrate) seeds, such as millets (especially millet spray), canary grass seed, oats, wheat, sweet corn, and rice. These must make up 80 to 90 percent of the total seed mixture. Oily seeds, such as sunflower, safflower, peanuts (which, incidentally, are not truly nuts but pod fruits), hemp, flax, niger, buckwheat, and poppy, should make up 15 to 20 percent of the seed mixture. In my experience, millet seeds

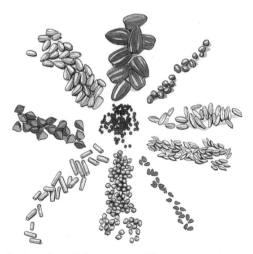

Seeds, pellets, fruits and vegetables are some of the conures' nutritional requirements. Clockwise from top: striped sunflower seed, hemp seed, oats, canary grass seed, flax seed, white millet, bird pellets, buckwheat, and safflower; center: rape seed.

Feeding

Conures appreciate a variety of green food and fruits.

are not as acceptable to conures as the other seeds, except for millet spray, which should be included in the diet, especially during the breeding season. Corn is also frequently ignored, and canary grass seed, flax, and poppy may not be taken by all conures. Corn is preferably taken if it has been softened (soaked).

In contrast, all conures are crazy about half-ripe weed seeds, which you can collect in the open field (make sure that they are not tainted with insecticides or other chemical sprays). You can freeze some of these in plastic bags for use in the winter (thawed out first, of course). Conures also appreciate germinated seeds of all kinds. Barely sprouted seeds are richest in vitamins, and they should be offered (especially sunflower seeds) in the breeding season. I give my birds about twenty sprouted sunflower seeds each per day in the aviary and about ten per day in the cage.

Conures also appreciate green food. Spinach, watercress, and field lettuce are eaten eagerly. Common lettuce has a high water content and should not be given in large quantities, as it can cause intestinal disturbances. Poppy, chickweed, and dandelions (including the roots) are always welcome and may be given throughout the year.

Since conures are gnawers, they should be given a regular supply of fresh twigs from willow, elder, hawthorn, poplar and fruit trees. Fruit can include berries, apples, pears, cherries, grapes, bananas and pieces of coconut. The fruit flesh must be visible (peeled and sliced), otherwise the birds won't eat it. As with seeds, not all conures will like all kinds of fruit offered. It took two years before some of my birds would try berries or strawberries. Many kinds of nuts may also not be accepted; experiment to see which kinds are acceptable. Nuts should be shelled, though peanuts can be left in the shell.

My birds get much pleasure if I offer them various insects (mealworms, aphids, white worms). But here, too, you may also find some conures that do not go head-over-heels for mealworms. Only time will tell what your birds will eventually decide is good for them. In the breeding season I offer insects mixed with egg food, as it is recognized that the protein provided by live food and egg (or universal) food is vital for many birds if they are to breed successfully and produce healthy young. This must be controlled carefully, especially in warm weather, when the food can spoil quickly.

Mineral and vitamin supplements can be sprinkled in powder form over fruit or green food; mineral blocks are also very useful. Minerals play an important role in the lives of conures. Certain *Pyrrhura* species, for example, live in the Barreiros, places with rich mineral holding earths (especially sodium), which are eaten by the birds. Cuttlefish bone is also a useful source of minerals, and as a beak conditioner.

Finally, always ensure availability of fresh drinking water. On warm days it should be replaced several times. The same goes for bathing water, but do not let the birds bathe in winter.

Feeding

Pellets

In recent years serious attempts have been made to improve the standard of pet bird feeding. There has been a tendency to adopt European methods—favoring a far more representative diet—with more emphasis on energy-producing ingredients and less concern for high protein content. Artificially enriched grains have also been tried.

From 1985 to 1991 an ambitious research program was carried out in which the problem of pet bird feeding was examined in depth at various food production centers. The result is the bird pellet, which is balanced in proteins and carbohydrates, comes in various fruit flavors and attractive colors and shapes, and is fortified with *Lactobacillus acidophilus* and yeast cultures in order to prevent the depletion of beneficial gut microbes and maintain normal intestinal conditions.

Feeding Instructions for Pellets: Blend the new diet with the old (seed) mixture and gradually reduce the old diet over a period of 16 days as follows:

Days 1 through 4: 25% pellets and 75% current seed mix.

Days 5 through 10: 50% pellets and 50% current seed mix.

Days 11 through 15: 75% pellets and 25% current seed mix.

Day 16: 100% pellets.

Moistening with fruit juice may help the birds in adjusting to the new pelleted diet, but wet food should be removed after four hours and replaced with clean, dry food. After 16 days the birds should be completely converted to pellets. If your birds are difficult to convert, return to the first step in the conversion process.

Most pellets are nutritionally balanced and designed to be fed as the sole diet. However, offer fresh fruits and vegetables daily in small amounts as well as treats and a variety of bird seeds. Keep food fresh by filling the feeders daily. Food should be available at all times. Clean feeders at least every other day to prevent mold, and refill with fresh pellets. Keep waterers clean, and have fresh water available at all times.

Diseases

Conures kept under optimum conditions and given a balanced diet are remarkably resistant to disease, and you should rarely have any problems. However, sickness may occasionally break out, and you must take this in stride. The bird, unfortunately, cannot tell us when there is something wrong or what is wrong with it. You must therefore be observant and try to diagnose the problem from the symptoms that are presented. You may often require the assistance of an avian veterinarian.

The bird fancy is still in its infancy when it comes to the prevention and treatment of sick birds. One reason is that there are far too few veterinarians with avian experience or qualifications. Another is that fanciers often shrug their shoulders when a bird dies and get another bird; they do not get an autopsy performed on the body to find out more about the disease that killed their bird. Other fanciers never bother to consult a veterinarian at all. So we sit in a sort of vicious circle. Fanciers don't consult their vets, so few vets are interested or specialized in avicultural matters.

Fortunately, some progress is being made, but it is very slow. All fanciers could help speed up the process by seeking out an avian veterinarian more often and encouraging their colleagues to do the same. Over a protracted period we can only profit from this strategy of sharing mutual experiences.

Every fancier should know something about bird disease. If you do not know enough, you can usually gain more information from a veterinarian or from a more experienced colleague. But this may not always be possible at a particular time, or you may need to take immediate action with a particular bird. So, if you know a little, you will at least be able to take some kind of action. What follows is a kind of first aid.

Ensure that all cages and aviaries are kept clean and that birds are free of pests and parasites such as mites and lice. A suitable (livestock-safe) insecticide should be kept for treatment if necessary.

The following items should be available in the house in case of illness or injury:

- A catching net and perhaps gloves. It is better to hold conures *without* gloves if possible, as you can then feel them better.
- A hospital cage or a wire cage with an infrared lamp. Priority first aid for a sick bird is warmth, preferably 86 to 95° F (30–35° C). A hospital cage has the disadvantage that it is frequently almost airtight, thus dry and stuffy with a constant temperature. A wire cage with an infrared lamp is airy, and the bird can move toward or away from the lamp as it wishes, thus choosing its *preferred* temperature. The brightness of an infrared lamp can be adjusted, and a thermostat can be used to control the temperature.
- A bleeding inhibitor (styptic), such as hydrogen peroxide (3 percent), in case of wounds.

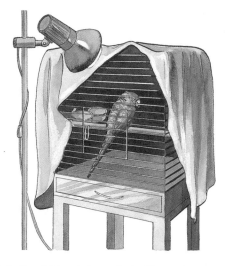

A "self-made" hospital cage. Preferably use a heat source that does not emit any light so that light levels can be regulated separately. An infrared lamp is also excellent as its brightness can be adjusted. A thermostat should be used to control the temperature; a thermometer is therefore essential but place it where the bird cannot reach it!

Diseases

- A pipette or syringe to administer medicine. The best is a syringe with a tube attached so that you can be sure the bird gets its full dose. You can get this from a veterinarian.
- A broad-spectrum antibiotic such as tetracycline HCl. Antibiotics come in various forms and they do not all work against the same microorganisms. If you use a broad-spectrum antibiotic (one which treats a range of organisms), you will have the best chance of securing a cure. However, if you do not know precisely what you are treating, it is best to consult a veterinarian.
- A vermicidal medium. Birds are susceptible to various kinds of worm infection. At one time some of these infections could be fatal. Today, however, there are excellent medicines that can

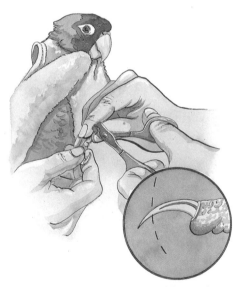

Clipping nails. The first step is to properly restrain your bird in a towel. The second step is to identify the blood vessel or quick, visible in light-colored nails as a red streak. Don't cut the quick, but if the claw does start to bleed, a moistened styptic pencil, silver nitrate, iron subsulfate or liquid coagulant should be applied to the bleeding end.

be administered regularly. Your veterinarian will advise you on this matter.
- One or more good books dealing with bird diseases and avian medicine (ask your veterinarian for appropriate titles). These books are not so much to be used to help owners treat and medicate their birds, but also to enable them to adequately describe symptoms and problems to the veterinarian.

A Bird's-Eye View of Some Diseases and Injuries

Aspergillosis, a respiratory infection, is caused by breathing spores of the fungus *Aspergillus fumigatus.* The bird shows symptoms of heavy breathing and tail bobbing. Prevent spores (from moldy bread, seeds, musty hay, etc.) from blowing into cage and aviary. Disinfect housing by spraying with a solution of 1% copper sulfate before any birds are replaced. Generally, all the birds will need to be sacrificed.

Candidiasis (an infection with *Candida* yeast) usually affects the surface of the mouth and crop of young, hand-reared birds. Candidiasis is probably due to vitamin A deficiency, which weakens the integrity of the surface tissue. Antifungal drugs and vitamin A injections are required for a fast recovery. Since seeds are poor in vitamin A, fresh vegetables (spinach, finely chopped dandelion, carrots) are essential in the conure's daily diet.

Top left: The sun conure (*Aratinga auricapillus solstitialis*), ▶ thinly distributed throughout its range, is often quite prolific in captivity.
Top right: The shape and size of the Queen of Bavaria conure (*A. guarouba*) doesn't resemble that of an Aratinga at all, but its playfulness is certainly characteristic of the genus.
Bottom: This young white-eyed conure (*A. l. leucophthalmus*) was raised in captivity. The species is rather rare in the wild.

Diseases

Colds and Sinus Inflammations frequently affect cage and aviary birds, as a result of drafts, temperature differences, vitamin A deficiency, stress, and exposure to various bacteria, fungi, and viruses. Birds exhibit nasal discharge, runny eyes, and sneezing. Affected eyes often have the tendency to close (look droopy). Sick birds require immediate veterinary attention and—often—vitamin A injections.

Diarrhea is not a disease but a clinical sign—a symptom. It accompanies a great many diseases and therefore should not be treated without first obtaining a correct diagnosis from an avian veterinarian, Don't confuse diarrhea with excess urinary output (polyuria). Place the bird in a hospital cage at 90° F (32° C) and give it antibiotics as advised by your avian veterinarian.

Egg Binding—caused by oversized or soft-shelled eggs, stress, muscle weakness in the oviduct (often due to old age), low blood calcium and glucose, overbreeding, or disease—should always be regarded as an emergency. Immediate veterinary attention is required. The symptoms of egg binding are easy to discern. The hen has ruffled feathers and usually sits on the bottom of the cage or aviary, breathing heavily. Place the bird in a hospital cage at 90° F (32° C). A *small* quantity of olive oil or lubricating jelly, introduced in the vent by means of a small brush or cotton swab, may bring some relief. Consult your avian vet without delay.

Egg Pecking is often the result of a lack of calcium—or boredom. Supply cuttlefish bone,

Clipping both wings as indicated (hence, leaving the two outermost primary flight feathers intact) may prevent serious injury in pet birds.

eggshell, and vitamin A and D. Replace the real eggs with artificial ones, and correct your feeding strategies.

Eye Infections need immediate veterinary attention. Clean each eye gently with a soft cotton swab and apply an antibiotic such as doxycycline.

Feather Plucking is usually the result of vitamin deficiency, listlessness, boredom, or overcrowding. Inspect your feeding program carefully and make the necessary corrections. Boredom and listlessness can be alleviated by supplying fresh twigs, toys, sisal rope, and a few bunches of millet spray or weed seed. Consult your vet, since steroids, tranquilizers, or hormones are usually required to correct the problem.

Frostbite: Freezing toes affect small conures in particular; their toes become frozen at 30° F (–2° C). Move the birds to a frost-free (but not too warm) room. However, the chances of the toes healing properly are almost nil. This should not stop you from doing all you can to help the birds.

Top left: The brown-throated conure (*Aratinga pertinax aeruginosa*) is an excellent breeder in captivity. Sometimes budgerigars are successfully used as foster parents.
Top right: The cactus conure (*A. c. cactorum*) is well-known in captivity. Due to its trustworthy temperament it often becomes an excellent pet.
Bottom left and right: The nanday conure (*A. or Nandayus nenday*) is a fairly prolific bird in captivity. Due to habitat loss, the wild population is diminishing.

Sometimes, particularly if the problem is caught in time, a massage with some Vaseline can help restore the blood circulation and thus regenerate the tissues. Consult your vet!

Goiter or Enlargement of the Thyroid Gland is found mainly in areas where drinking water is deficient in iodine. Provide an iodine-glycerin mixture of one part iodine to four parts glycerine. Various mineral blocks, which are available in pet shops, contain iodine and will help prevent this problem effectively.

Mites, at least the external parasites, are common in birds. *Cnemidocoptic* mites burrow into the skin around the beak, eyelids, legs, and feet and are responsible for scaly face and scaly leg disease. Apply benzylbenzoate or Eurax cream while your vet treats the bird with a systemic insecticide (Invermectin, or Equalan), an injectable medication.

Red or gray mites (*Dermanyssus gallinae* or *D. avium*) are a real problem. They come at night in great numbers, sit on the birds, and suck blood. The only way to exterminate these pests and avoid recurring visits is a regular and careful control of cleanliness. Inspect the nest boxes, utensils, perches, and cracks or crevices for signs of mites. Many effective insecticides are available at your pet shop. Skin and feather mites (*Syringophilus bipectioratus* and *Dermoglyphus elongatus*) require the same treatment.

Pacheco's Disease is a massive problem in the United States. It is caused by a strain-specific virus and is primarily seen in areas where many birds are kept, such as quarantine stations, pet shops, and zoos, or in birds coming from such places. The bird suffers from stress, diarrhea, depression, and appetite loss. Nanday conures (page 67) and Patagonian conures (page 73) are suspected of being carriers, transmitting this deadly disease to other birds, although poultry, mynah birds, finches, and canaries (and humans) appear not to be susceptible to it.

Psittacosis is caused by an intracellular parasite, *Chlamydia psittaci*. Affected birds do not want to eat, fluff up their feahers, gasp for air while moisture drips from their nostrils, and their droppings are gray-green in color. The final stage of the disease is marked by nervous disorders. For example, birds can no longer sit on their perches. Imported birds have to be quarantined for 30 days upon arrival and are given food with chlortetracycline. Infected birds are treated for 45 days with this drug, but chances of recovery usually are slim, with the affected birds dying quickly. Consult your avian vet immediately. Remember: human beings can contract this serious disease, too!

Salmonella is caused by bacteria that can pose serious problems for your birds. The affected birds lose all interest in food and suffer from diarrhea, painful joints, and nervous disorders.

Contact your vet immediately.

Worms: This is a problem with which practically every bird keeper is confronted sooner or later. The two culprits are:
- Roundworms *(Ascaris)*, fiber-thin white worms, about 8 inches (3.2 cm) long, that live in the upper part of the intestinal tract.
- Threadworms *(Capillaria)*, extremely thin and transparent worms that also live in the intestines, surrounded by the catarrhal slime engendered by their irritating effect on the intestinal wall.

Both worms are true parasites: only the eggs can survive outside the host body. Worms driven out with an antiworm treatment prescribed by your vet *(Piperzine, Levamisole)* die quickly and are no longer infectious. Extreme precaution, however, must be taken with various antiworm medications, as they are basically poisonous. Dosage is directly related to body weight, and, if too much is used, the bird can become ill or even die.

The only way to prevent these pests or avoid recurring visits is regular and careful control of cleanliness. Regular stool examinations by your avian veterinarian are advisable.

Understanding Conures

Getting Acquainted

Conures are extremely varied birds. However, all conures have a fairly broad cere at the base of the beak. Their moderately sturdy beaks are never red in color; the most common colors are black and a light horn color.

Conures fall into one of the following categories: birds with short tails that become narrower at the tip and birds with long, slender tails. Practically all species have a clearly defined eye ring, which can be very helpful in determining the sex outside the breeding season; females generally have a somewhat narrower ring than the males.

Aratinga: The genus *Aratinga* is increasingly more popular with aviculturists. There is some disagreement among ornithologists about the number of species and subspecies in this genus. Thus the number of species varies between 15 and 21, while there may be 53 to 57 subspecies, depending on individual opinions. This book follows the classification used by Joseph Forshaw in the third edition of his *Parrots of the World*. According to him, there are 19 species and 35 subspecies (of which one is now extinct). There are seven species without subspecies, while the St. Thomas conure has 13 subspecies in addition to the type subspecies.

Cocks and hens are outwardly very similar in appearance, although I believe that hens possess a grayer iris than cocks. But to make such distinctions you need to have adequate comparative material. According to some aviculturists, the hens also have a somewhat coarser head. According to the late Mrs. J. Spenkelink van Schaik, the sexual differences of *Aratinga* species are similar to those of macaws: the feathers on the edge of the forehead and between the nostrils and eyes are longer and wider in the cocks than in the hens, giving the effect of eyebrows. In cocks the curve of the beak is stronger than in the hens, giving the appearance of a hump on the upper beak. In the hens the beak *looks* longer, but measurements prove that this is an optical illusion!

Aratinga species dig holes or use rock crevices, tree hollows, termite nests, and tunnels in river banks for nesting sites. The female lays three to eight eggs, which she alone broods for about 27 days. The male often joins his mate in the nest for the evening and night. The young leave the nest at about 50 days of age, but the parents still care for their young a considerable time after that.

Brotogeris: The genus *Brotogeris* has seven species and 15 subspecies. The sexes are hard to differentiate. They all have a typical narrow, pointed, protruding bill with a wide, rounded notch in the upper mandible. Their diet in the wild consists of seeds, maggots, small worms, and ant pupae. In captivity they like canary rearing food, stale bread soaked in water and squeezed out, canary grass seed, hemp, various millets, millet spray, small black sunflowers, pieces of sweet apple, halved oranges, grapes, pears, bananas, grapefruit, and berries. A good variety of green food (at all times, but especially in the breeding season) and germinated seeds are essential.

Breeding successes with these birds are few. Since the purchase price of the birds is relatively low, fanciers may not try too hard! The birds do not require a large aviary, though they do not seem to relish cage life. It is recommended that each pair be kept separately. In the wild the birds nest in termite nests and trees, almost always in rather large groups. The female lays four to six eggs in a hollow, and she broods them for about 26 days. After about two months, the young leave the nest.

Enicognathus: The genus *Enicognathus* includes two currently quite popular species, the slender-billed conure and the austral conure. Both come from southern South America.

Cyanoliseus: The Patagonian conure and its three subspecies belong to the genus *Cyanoliseus*. They usually nest in holes they dig themselves, with a passage that sometimes extends more than 10 feet (3 m). The female usually lays two eggs; incubation time is 25 days. After the young are hatched, the male commences to feed the offspring,

Understanding Conures

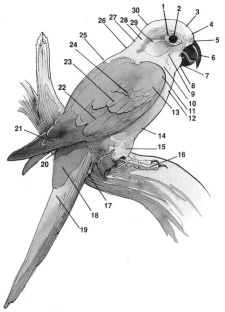

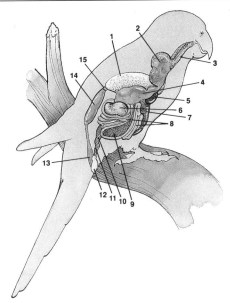

The internal anatomy of a conure: 1. lung, 2. crop, 3. esophagus, 4. proventriculus, 5. heart, 6. gizzard, 7. liver, 8. small intestine, 9. pancreas, 10. large intestine, 11. rectum, 12. cloaca, 13. ureter, 14. kidney, 15. adrenal gland.

Knowing the different parts of a conure's body is especially useful when talking with breeders, judges, and avian veterinarians: 1. eye ring, 2. iris, 3. crown, 4. forehead, 5. cere, 6. upper mandible, 7. lower mandible, 8. chin, 9. cheek, 10. neck, 11. bend of wing, 12. breast, 13. shoulder, 14. abdomen, 15. thigh, 16. toes, 17. undertail coverts, 18. uppertail coverts, 19. tail feathers, 20. rump, 21. primaries, 22. secondaries, 23. greater wing coverts, 24. median wing coverts, 25. back, 26. mantle, 27. nape, 28. back of neck, 29. ear coverts, 30. back of head

but also spends quite some time in the nest. These birds are very hardy and need a daily supply of fruit tree and willow twigs, as well as thick branches, to satisfy their desire to chew. Strong netting and an aviary of metal are essential.

Pyrrhura: The genus *Pyrrhura* includes 18 species of conures and 37 subspecies, many of which are kept in captivity today. In the wild the birds live on fruits, berries, blossom leaves, insects (and their eggs and larvae), and a rich assortment of seeds. The nest is usually in a tree hollow. The clutch consists of two to four eggs on the average,

but as many as eight have been recorded. The female alone broods the eggs, which hatch in 22 to 28 days. After about two months, the young leave the nest, but they are still fed thereafter, principally by their father.

Conures in the Wild

Conures can be found in most of South and Central America, and some species are also well represented in the West Indies. Some species, like the monk parakeet, inhabit even southeastern New York, New Jersey, and Connecticut, where the birds have been introduced; nests have been reported from Massachusetts, Virginia, and Florida.

In the wild conures are friendly, peaceful birds;

they seldom fight with each other. They live together in groups of twenty or more birds, even during the mating season, and feed on various seeds, fruits, and insects. However, they have been known to attack and eat smaller species of birds during migration in the fall.

Conures often do quite a lot of damage to planted fields; I have witnessed many cornfields that were picked clean completely. As a consequence, the birds are often shot down.

Vocal Abilities

The "voice" of many conures, unfortunately, is not always pleasant and often consists of a series of loud, somewhat raucous calls. In spite of their sometimes deafening calls (although the petite *Pyrrhura* and *Brotogeris* species are relatively quiet), they are extremely popular among bird fanciers, since many are delightful companions with lively, fearless character. Because of their pleasant and peaceful nature, many of the conures can become finger-tame in just a few weeks, providing they receive proper care.

My pair of canary-winged parakeets speak a few words in both English and Dutch, and my wife has taught them Shakespeare's "To be or not to be" from *Hamlet*. This phrase sounds incredibly funny when uttered in certain situations. In general, however, canary-winged parakeets are less talkative than the loving and gentle gray-cheeked conures which, incidentally, often form a strong, almost obsessive bond with their owner.

Some conure species "open their screeching mouth" when they are not accustomed to their new surroundings. After a few weeks in their aviary or roomy cage, they generally become much more peaceful and may even take food from your hand.

Red-fronted conures are some of the best talkers. My wife had a charming pair. Both sexes could quote a few lines (if not all that clearly) from the Bible and Keats' poems. These birds attracted a lot of attention and were so tame that they could accompany my wife on her way to college and remain in the trees by the school until she returned from class to pick them up.

Courtship Behavior

The breeding season in the wild depends mostly on the weather and availability of food; it can often last seven to eight months. Only one species, the monk parakeet, builds a traditional type of nest in trees or high shrubbery; the other conures nest in tree hollows (the nest box would be the counterpart in the aviary) or in rock crevices (in the aviary, a half-open nest box). Various *Brotogeris* species have their nests in termite mounds.

During courtship male conures start their courtship dance. Many species begin to gnaw at twigs, perches, and nest boxes at this time. Various species frequently spread the tail feathers and fluff out their head and neck feathers. *Pyrrhura* species form a little crest, while they nervously and excitedly dance back and forth along the perch. The white-winged parakeet *(Brotogeris v. versicolor)*, almost wholly green in color except for yellow and white patches on the wings, stretches out the wings so that the color patches are clearly visible to the partner. Many *Pyrrhura* and *Brotogeris* species preen each other's feathers for long periods, not only on the head but also on other parts of the body, which the bird could reach itself. Usually, only areas that a bird cannot reach by itself are preened by a partner.

During copulation, according to Rosemary Low, almost all psittacines place both feet on the back of the female; but, presumably, all the small neotropical parakeets (including *Aratinga* and *Pyrrhura* species) keep one foot on the perch. It is indeed remarkable how well the South American parakeets use their feet as "hands," with the exception of the *Forpus* species and the white-winged parakeet.

Breeding South American Conures

Introduction

The care and breeding of South American conures in captivity remains an adventure full of surprises. In the past not much effort was made to breed the birds, since one could easily get imported specimens at relatively low prices. Today, however, with emphasis on the conservation of wildlife (in some cases the total banning of collection from the wild and import prohibition), wild captured stock is scarce. Thus our breeding experience started fairly recently, and we still have much to learn.

The best breeding results are achieved with single true or proven pairs of birds kept in aviaries, with the exception of some of the smaller species. This is unfortunate, since many fanciers have limited space in which to house their birds. Even with adequate space, it is rather expensive to build large blocks of aviaries. *True pairs*, by the way, are birds that have actually been sexed, either by endoscopic examination, fecal testing, or genetic sexing. Pairs that have been visually sexed cannot be said to be true pairs. *Proven pairs* should be even better than true pairs, as these are birds that have bred and produced young. It is, however, very difficult to purchase proven pairs, as it is the equivalent of the seller giving up "the golden goose." However, South American conures can get by with less room than most Australian or African parakeets.

The most important thing is to work with *true pairs*. The most natural and best method of forming pairs is to place a group of birds together in a large aviary (this may require a cooperative effort with other bird owners). The birds will form pairs that later can be separated out.

It is good to keep a few "spare" birds in case any of these partnerships should break up. A big advantage of keeping two or more pairs in two or more aviaries is that you can keep inbreeding to a minimum and build unrelated lines.

Most South American conures (in fact, all those described in this book) do not require huge aviaries. I have had successful results with *Aratinga*,

Brotogerus, and *Pyrrhura* species in aviaries 9½ feet (3.5 m) long, 6 feet (2 m) high, and 3 feet (1 m) wide with a night shelter of 3½ feet (1.5 m). The night shelter is fitted with a sleeping board about 8 inches (20 cm) wide, fixed about 19½ inches (50 cm) below the ceiling. There is a choice of nest boxes, one of which will be chosen by the birds to sleep in and even to rest in during the day.

I also provide a number of shady spots in the shelter and in the flight; I have noticed that conures like to lurk in these at times. I believe that they feel more secure if they are concealed from prying eyes. Without such hiding places the birds are less likely to breed. There are examples of outstanding, spacious, light, and efficient aviaries that have done nothing for conure breeding. Aviaries without a lot of shade-giving shrubs planted around them must be regarded as unsuitable for neotropical parakeets.

Sex Determination

Successful reproduction requires a true pair (male and female) of birds. Unfortunately, it is very difficult to distinguish the sexes of most conure species by physical appearance. When purchasing a "pair," it is wise to get a signed guarantee that you can exchange one of them should they turn out to be of the same sex.

As suggested above, a number of birds can be placed in a large aviary and separated as they pair off.

However, you should be aware that South American parakeets, unlike Australian broad-tailed parakeets, show affection toward each other throughout the year, not just at breeding time. You must therefore not reach any quick conclusions if your conures show interest in each other, especially outside the breeding season. This does not necessarily mean that you have a true pair. Two hens or two cocks can just as easily set themselves up as a loving pair. Usually, however, you can tell

Breeding South American Conures

from the birds' behavior whether or not you have a true pair.

Physical Appearance

The sex of some conure species can be determined by color differences between males and females. In *Aratinga* species the green color can show different tones. In green and red *Aratinga* species the hens are somewhat less red than the cocks; this is fairly clear in the mitered conure *(A. mitrata)*, in which the hens show only a little red in the cheeks. Hens of the Jenday conure *(A. jandaya)* and the sun conure *(A. solstitialis)* are less orange than the cocks; moreover, the Jenday conure hen frequently shows some green on the breast. In the peach-fronted conure *(A. canicularis)* the orange forehead band of the female is smaller than that of the male. In spite of these differences, color is not a reliable method for sexing conures, since individuals within each species can show a considerable variety of color patterns, and no bird is the same as the next.

The shape and size of the head can often be a better indication. As a general rule, the hen's head (seen from the side) is smaller and rounder than that of the cock; the hen's beak is also slighter in build. The cock has a more angular skull with a smaller forehead and a more robust beak.

The body form—with sufficient comparative material—can also give some clues to the sex of a conure. Hens generally have a slighter and slimmer body form than cocks and are usually a little shorter in length. This is especially apparent in the wing and tail feathers, which are shorter in the hen than in the cock. However, these differences, too, are not a reliable means of distinguishing between the sexes, since other circumstances (age, food, lifestyle, breeding condition) can affect the development of individual birds.

Brotogeris species are extremely difficult to sex by outward appearance. An exception is the cobalt-winged conure *(B. c. cyanoptera)*, in which most hens (usually also more robust) have a somewhat duller yellow color on the forehead, which does not reach as far over the crown as in the cock.

Visible sexual characteristics are also poorly represented in *Pyrrhura* species. With the exception of *P. melanura, P. molinae,* and *P. rupicola,* which have a number of small sexual differences, cocks and hens are very similar (although the heads of the cocks may be a little more robust and flatter than those of the hens, and their beaks may be heavier and more highly arched).

Diagnostic Methods

Several diagnostic methods are now available to determine the sex of birds. Here are three of them.

Blood Test: This is a noninvasive procedure in which a single drop of blood is examined, and *no* general anesthetic is necessary. Since only a few laboratories carry out this test, you can obtain further information from the resident avian veterinarian of Zoogen Incorporated, 1105 Kennedy Place, Suite 4, Davis, California 95616.

Endoscopic Examination: Such an examination can be carried out only by a qualified avian veterinarian. Since many avian veterinarians are members of avicultural societies, they will usually do the examination for a reasonable price. The bird to be examined is anesthetized; the amount of anesthetic used will depend on the weight of the bird. The bird must have no food for several hours before the examination, so that the danger of regurgitation and suffocation is eliminated. After the examination the bird should be placed for several hours in a small cage in a warm, quiet area for it to recuperate.

The advantage of endoscopic examination is that it can determine much more than just the sex of a bird. By looking inside the bird's body, the vet can make observations about its health, breeding condition, maturity, etc. South American parakeets must be at least nine months old before an endoscopic examination is attempted. Before that time the partially developed sex organs will be difficult to find or recognize.

Breeding South American Conures

Pelvic Test: In this method, which is used extensively by breeders of lovebirds (Agapornidae), the width across the pubic arch determines male from female. The ends of the pubic bones may be palpated directly above the vent. In fully grown cocks these almost touch each other; in hens you can almost get your finger between them. It may also be noted that also, the ends of these bones are sharper and more pointed in cocks. The best way to carry out this examination is to grip the bird, with its belly upward, in one hand and to feel the width of the gap with the index finger of the other hand. I find this method rather unreliable, although it can give you some idea when buying new birds. It is advisable to select two birds with the greatest width differences to ensure a true pair. The distance between the tips of the pubic bones varies from individual to individual, especially with hens. It is at its widest during egg laying and at breeding time. But there is little difference between cocks and hens at other times or when the hens are young. Fanciers with years of experience may find this method reasonably reliable, but, in general, it is best to rely on an endoscopic examination if you want to be certain.

Aratinga Species

Outside the breeding season wild *Aratinga* conures move about in small—but sometimes moderately large—groups. During the breeding season they separate into pairs—with the exception of the *Aratinga pertinax* group (the St. Thomas conure, the brown-throated conure, and the brown-eared conure, for example) and *Aratinga wagleri*, the red-fronted conure. Climatic factors and availability of food influence the time of pairing, but these factors in subtropical Central and South America are nowhere near as dramatic as the seasonal changes in most parts of temperate North America and Europe.

Not all *Aratinga* conures nest in hollow tree trunks or branches, although such sites seem to be preferred to holes in the ground. Some pairs raise their families in hollowed-out termite nests (these are frequently in trees), rock crevices, hollow cactus stems, and so on.

Members of the *Aratinga* genus have a very simple courtship ceremony. Apart from actual copulation, mutual feeding seems to be the only nuptial behavior. During feeding the feathers may be fluffed out and the hen may occasionally let out an enthusiastic call. This behavior can become quite intensive and stretch over a long period. Feeding is proof that the birds are interested in each other; it will usually culminate in pairing. Unlike Australian parakeets, for example, male conures never pursue their hens in frantic passion.

Selection of Breeding Pairs

In general, most *Aratinga* conures will readily accept a partner. However, this is not always the case. Successful breeding results occur only if the birds get along well with each other. Birds that are interested in each other preen each other's feathers, follow each other around in the aviary, and sleep by each other on a perch. My observations of various *Aratinga* species have shown that birds that sleep together are likely to become an ideal breeding pair. I have seen birds that got along very well in a community aviary but never slept together; such birds never paired with each other.

The best way to get good pairs is to place a group of birds (of the same species and age) in a large aviary and allow them to pair off. Such pairs are most likely to produce the best breeding results. With this method you must be able to identify each bird individually. Colored leg bands are an ideal method of identifying individual birds. If you wish to be efficient with your breeding stock, individual identification of birds is essential.

If you bring two birds together it does not necessarily mean that they will breed successfully in the first season. It can sometimes take a few years before the first eggs are laid. Sometimes two

Breeding South American Conures

birds that apparently get along very well never form a breeding pair. In such cases it is best to separate them and try to pair them with other individuals. However, always give the birds a fair amount of time to prove themselves before taking any drastic action.

Accommodation and food plays an important part in the forming of pairs. An aviary that is subjected to constant pandemonium (such as domestic arguments, tumultuous parties, barking dogs, unruly children, ear-splitting music, and loud visitors) will seldom produce breeding pairs.

Newly imported birds may take several years to settle into the aviary community. Young birds become accustomed to new surrounding faster than older ones. Birds that have been together for a number of years in an aviary usually will not accept strange birds. Therefore, it is best to form new groups with young birds, which have not yet formed social bonds with other birds.

You must take great care in introducing a new partner to a bird that has lost its original partner. The bird that has lost its partner should be left *alone* in the original aviary for a week to ten days. After that a new partner may be carefully introduced. Hopefully, by then the lost partner will be forgotten and the new one will be readily accepted.

Housing and Nest Boxes

Home-bred birds pose fewer problems than those imported from their country of origin or from other countries where they have been bred in captivity. In any case birds must be kept in such a manner that they feel safe and contented. Keeping several pairs of the same species is a good inducement for most pairs to breed, especially if they can see and hear each other. However, it is not recommended that pairs be accommodated in adjacent aviaries, where squabbling can be detrimental to breeding.

Although experience has shown that best results usually occur when pairs are housed separately, there are exceptions when it is possible to keep several pairs (always three or more) in a community aviary. But beware of overcrowding. As a general rule, each pair should have at least 4 square yards (about 3.5 m²) of ground area. Outside the breeding season Jenday and golden conures for example, can be housed together in groups; these species are friendly and tolerate each other well. But you must have large aviaries for such groups, since both species require a lot of room. Many golden conures (especially in the United States) are bred in relatively small cages; the nest box usually is outside the cage, attached to one of the sides, so that inspection is easy.

Although conures are gregarious birds, they do have a "pecking order." Thus the strongest birds are the first to breed. They get the best nest boxes—usually those farthest from the aviary entrance, and thus the quietest and safest. The weaker birds get second choice and may be less successful. As already noted, aviaries and flights placed adjacent to each other sometimes pose problems, especially if they contain pairs of the same species. If you have no other choice, the adjoining aviary walls should be double meshed, with a space of at least 1¼ inches (3 cm) between the wire, so that the birds cannot reach each other to bite (which they like to try—believe me!).

In general aratingas must be 18 months to two years old before they are sexually mature. Some species, such as the sun conures, must be over two years old before they can breed, and some of the larger species must be three to four years old.

As noted earlier, aratingas have no specific courtship behavior, but they do develop a strong pair bond (whereby the cock feeds the hen). The hen enters the nest box approximately three weeks before laying the first eggs; the cock may join her 7 to 14 days later.

The birds (mainly the hen) gnaw the lining of the box, especially the floor, to such an extent that the whole floor may be destroyed after a few weeks. Of course, any eggs in the nest would fall and break on the aviary floor. It is therefore very important to have a very thick floor or a double floor; the latter should have an inner layer of wood and an outer layer of mesh or metal. Ensure that you can open the top of the nest box for inspection. I personally prefer nest boxes with an inspection door on the side, to the left or right of the entrance hole, making it easy to control.

Make the nest boxes from plywood approximately ½ to ¾ inch (1.5–2 cm) thick, so that a relatively constant temperature can be maintained. For the smaller species a box 14 inches long, 10 inches wide, and 15 inches high (35 x 25 x 30 cm) is ideal, while larger species require a box 24 inches long, 16 inches wide, and 16 inches high (60 x 40 x 40 cm); an inch more or less is not important. The entrance hole should be 2 to 2½ inches (5–6 cm) for the smaller and 2½ to 3½ inches (6–8 cm) for the larger species. Once a hen picks a particular nest box, whatever the size, she will gnaw the entrance hole to a suitable diameter.

You should also consider so-called natural nest logs for aratingas. Their thick walls will protect the birds from sudden temperature changes. It is preferable to use oak or beech logs, which are better able to withstand an onslaught of gnawing than those of softwood (for example, the birch boxes available in pet stores for budgerigars and cockatiels). For the smaller species, the natural nest box should have a minimum diameter of 8 inches (20 cm) with a height of 10 inches (25 cm); larger species require a diameter of 16 to 18 inches (40–45 cm) and a height of 14 inches (35 cm). Natural logs are difficult to inspect, though I have seen logs with a side door as well as a removable top. Some manufacturers have produced nest boxes made of metal that are T-shaped, L-shaped, and even Z-shaped. These odd shapes prevent damage to eggs if the hen or cock should enter the nest box rapidly; they also permit the hen to move to safety away from the male if he should suddenly become aggressive.

The floor of the nest box should be covered with a 2-inch (5-cm) layer of wood shavings or chips, peat, or wood pulp. Mix some damp earth

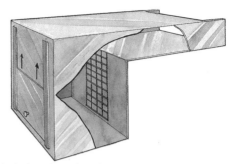

An L-shaped metal nest box, as used by the author. Note the internal wire mesh ladder enabling the parents and their young to climb in and out easily.

with the mulm in order to minimize drying out. Wood pulp gets dusty if allowed to dry out and can cause respiratory problems (aspergillosis, for example). Do not be surprised if a hen prefers to deposit her eggs on a bare floor, after having removed all the nest material. The eggs will usually end up on a bed of splinters anyway, originating from the hen's gnawing on the nest box lining. After the full clutch of eggs has been laid, gnawing may decrease or stop altogether.

Coarse sawdust can also be used as nest material (fine sawdust is too dusty and can get in the eyes and nostrils of the young). I have also had success with grass sod, about 2 inches (5 cm) thick, laid *upside down* on the floor of the nest box. Whatever material you use, try to make a nest hollow by pressing down with your fist. Some fanciers like to collect rotten timber, dead leaves, or pine needles from the woods and use this as an excellent moisture-holding nest material.

I have discovered that a choice of nest boxes ensures a greater chance of success. Similar types of boxes should be placed in the shelter and in the flight. One in the shelter is usually preferred, since the birds like to raise a family in peace and quiet and hate to be disturbed. In time you will know exactly what your birds prefer.

Breeding South American Conures

Do not be surprised if the birds choose the smallest nest box you have offered. The entrance hole must be just wide enough for the adult bird to pass through. If the entrance is too wide or the box itself too large, it will usually be rejected. A nest box that admits too much daylight makes a bird feel unsafe. It is therefore best to face the entrance hole of the box away from the strongest light sources, especially from direct sunlight and from the aviary entrance.

Pairing (frequently after several days of feeding by the cock), is accomplished in a typical manner: the cock sits next to the hen on a perch, sets one foot on her back, and brings his lower body under hers. Some individuals may even pair in the nest box.

Brooding, Hatching, and Rearing the Young

The start of brooding can vary from pair to pair; one hen may start with the first egg, another after the third. In most cases it is somewhere in between. The cock stays close to the nest and keeps the hen company, sometimes even spending the night with her in the box. He does not take part in the brooding.

The clutch averages three to four eggs; for the smaller species it can be as many as seven. In general, they are laid every other day, occasionally every third day. The white eggs vary from 20 x 30 millimeters in the orange-fronted conure *(A.c. canicularis)* to 26 x 35 millimeters in the golden conure *(A. guarouba)*. In the wild if *Aratinga* nests are visited by snakes or egg-eating mammals, the birds start a new brood somewhere else if the rainy season is not over. Some species raise two or more broods per season as a rule.

The hen incubates alone, but the cock usually stays close by, sometimes sitting in the entrance hole, or spending the night in the nest keeping the hen company. Sometimes he may even go into the nest during the day. During this period the birds are very sensitive to disturbances and may abandon eggs and young almost at the drop of a hat. You must take extreme caution not to disturb the birds when inspecting a nest.

A fertile egg becomes darker during incubation. After one to five days, blood vessels begin to develop; these can be seen if the egg is held in front of a strong light. The darker the surroundings, the easier it is to see the blood vessels.

Under normal conditions the fertile eggs hatch after 23 to 25 days. However, there can be exceptions. For example, the hen may leave the eggs at night for one reason or another. If she is away too long, the eggs will cool too much and the embryos will die. A young hen with an insufficiently developed brooding instinct may not incubate the eggs properly. Either of the adults may carry a pathogen that can be passed to the eggs.

A crack or hole in the eggshell can cause it to dry out. If you discover this in time, you can help by painting clear nail polish over the damaged area, thus making it airtight again. Return the egg to the nest only after the polish has thoroughly set, otherwise the egg may stick to the hen's feathers. Sometimes an egg can dry out if the shell is too thin or too porous. This can usually be avoided if the birds receive adequate calcium in the diet. An inadequate diet may also produce weak embryos that cannot break out of the eggshell. This can also occur if humidity is low, as in long spells of hot, dry weather.

If hens refuse to incubate their eggs, it is worth considering the use of a foster parent. Ideally, this should be another conure that has already laid eggs. An incubator can also be used but it is much easier to have the birds incubate the eggs themselves. If the parents appear to damage or destroy their eggs, incubator hatching can save the eggs.

If you think an egg is taking too long to hatch, you can apply a simple test to see if the embryo is still alive. Place the egg gently—and for only a few seconds—in lukewarm water. If the embryo is still alive, the egg will move about; if the egg does not move, the embryo is dead.

Don't worry if a pipped egg takes a while to

hatch. It can take as long as 48 hours from the appearance of the first crack in the shell to full hatching. Don't forget that this is a strenuous job for such a tiny creature—so give it time! If you hold the egg to your ear, you may hear the baby bird chirping softly. Don't try to help; birds that have been helped to hatch often don't make it. Let nature take its course if at all possible.

Don't worry if the newly hatched young have no food in their crops for some time. A hatchling has enough nourishment from the egg yolk to last it at least 12 hours. Thus hatchlings are not fed by the parents at first.

Newly born young are pinkish in color with whitish down. The eyes remain closed and begin to open after the twelfth day. At 10 to 14 days dark feather shafts begin to appear under the skin, and the legs and beak begin to darken. After three to four weeks, feather colors begin to appear, and the birds become fully feathered after about seven weeks. At this time the young are ready to leave the nest. The exact time depends on the weather and on their food.

It is best to leave the young with their parents until they are fully grown. But if the hen lays a second clutch there is a danger that the eggs will be broken, since the entire family likes to spend the night in the nest box. Therefore, remove the young and accommodate them out of sight and sound of the parents. After about 10 days (when parents and young no longer recognize each other) they can be accommodated near each other in separate aviaries. Never move a breeding pair to another aviary, since this will interrupt the breeding rhythm; it is always the young that should be moved.

A word of caution about the behavior of a hen with eggs or young: she can be extremely aggressive at this time and may even attack you if you enter the aviary. Golden conures have an especially bad reputation. You can easily hear the young when they are being fed by the mother. When inspecting the young (possible only when the hen is away from the nest), you will notice that they

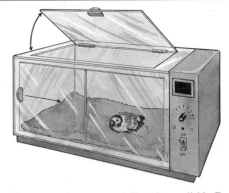

There are various commercial brooders available. For the first few days—when the young are still very small—the temperature should be maintained at 99.5° F (37.5° C). The temperature may be reduced gradually as the young increase in weight but do not allow it to drop to below 86° F (30° C) until they are ready to be acclimatized to lower temperatures. The brooder temperature should be controlled preferably with a thermostat because young birds are unable to tolerate sudden temperature changes.

usually huddle close to each other, thus conserving warmth.

During the breeding season, extra sweet corn, oats, and hemp (which are high in protein and vitamin E) should be given. Minerals (cuttlebone, mineral blocks, etc.) must also be available.

Aratingas occasionally bite and eat their eggs. This usually means that the bird is deficient in calcium, protein, or vitamins. If your birds peck at their eggs, you should do as follows: remove any damaged eggs from the nest box and foster them out or hatch them in an incubator. Replace the real eggs with artificial eggs. When the removed eggs are ready to hatch, put them back into the nest box and remove the artificial ones. The hatching and rearing process will then usually proceed without difficulty.

Nest Inspection

Fanciers have various answers to the question of how frequently nest boxes should be inspected.

Breeding South American Conures

It is not necessary to make your own rearing diets as there are balanced commercial diets available; all of these come with detailed instructions. A syringe or plastic dropper can be used to administer the food.

I do it quite frequently, but never to the extent that the birds are scared off the eggs. It is important to know the character and behavior of each of your breeding pairs and to regulate your nest inspections accordingly. Thus proceed with utmost caution with shy birds or with those that are breeding for the first time.

The main advantage of nest inspections is that if anything is wrong, you will be able to do something about it immediately. An egg may be cracked or may have rolled into a corner of the box. Eggs may not be incubated properly, or the young may be inadequately fed. Infertile eggs should be removed as soon as they have been identified. There is no point in letting a hen waste three weeks sitting on infertile eggs.

It is wise to have an incubator available for emergencies. If a hen fails to do her duty or has too many eggs, you can place the eggs in the incubator. If things improve, the eggs can always be returned to the hen. The temperature of the incubator should be between 99.4 and 100.5°F (37.4–38°C). An alternative to the incubator is to use suitable foster parents.

Brotogeris Species

In the wild most *Brotogeris* species breed in hollow limbs, especially in termite nests, found in a variety of trees. Depending on the weather and availability of food, the breeding season can last for seven to eight months. Outside the breeding season most species form large foraging groups. A few species remain fairly sociable even during the breeding season.

Breeding birds in captivity normally is not difficult, especially if each pair has its own roomy aviary with night shelter. Some species, especially the white- and yellow-winged conures, also breed well in a large cage. This is because many *Brotogeris* species become very tame and trusting toward humans. However, disturbances during breeding should still be kept to a minimum. The more peaceful the surroundings, the greater the chance of success.

Selection of Breeding Pairs

The best pairs are obtained when birds are allowed to choose their own partners. This can be achieved by cooperation among fanciers (see *Aratinga* species, page 36). It is not recommended that you keep more than one pair in an aviary since the birds can interfere with each others' nests, eggs, or young. In community aviaries stronger birds are likely to drive the weaker ones off their nests and peck the eggs, even eating them or killing the young. It is thus best to give each pair its own flight and shelter. Keep pairs in adjoining cages so that they can see and hear each other. This gives the birds an added impetus to breed. In the wild these birds live in colonies (outside the breeding season) and have strong social ties. The mesh between the flights should be double with a gap of about 1 inch (2.5 cm), so that the birds cannot injure each other.

Housing and Nest Boxes

Best breeding results are obtained with natural beech or oak nest boxes (available in pet shops),

Breeding South American Conures

which must have a minimum diameter of 7 to 8 inches (18–20 cm). Many natural log nests supplied for budgerigars or cockatiels will also do well for these charming South American birds. Place the nesting logs in a secluded, shady spot high up in the shelter or flight. Each pair should have a choice of at least three boxes, placed in different spots. You can also use nest boxes of hardwood boards at least ½ inch (1.5 cm) thick. These will be discussed in more detail in the next chapter.

The nesting facilities should have a false floor, forming two chambers (see page 37). In Europe, molded concrete nest boxes are used. These have a "foyer" accessed by a 2-inch-long (5 cm) entrance about 3¼ inches (8 cm) in diameter. There is another entrance of similar size from the "foyer" to the brooding chamber, which is about 8 inches (20 cm) in diameter. Such nest boxes are heavy to handle and difficult to inspect, but they are readily accepted by many species—probably because they are similar to the termite nests used in the wild.

The smaller species are sexually mature at eight to nine months. During courtship the partners feed each other (see *Aratinga* species, page 36), begin to gnaw at the nest box, and the cock tries to impress the hen with body gestures. Both sexes (but especially the hen) become aggressive toward the fancier. During copulation the cock places one foot on the hen's back.

Most broods are reared in the spring (middle of April to May), but this is by no means a general rule. These birds can breed at any time of the year as long as a good nest box and optimum conditions are available.

As a rule, the birds rear two or three broods per season. Young *Brotogeris* species are more or less independent about two to three weeks after fledging, but should still be left for another one to two weeks with their parents who will teach them a few more tricks about staying alive. In the fifth week after fledging, the young must be separated from the adults before the latter become aggressive toward them. Pairs wanting to nest again have been

known to kill their previous broods—so beware! Remove the earlier young as soon as they are independent (about two to three weeks), so that the hen can start undisturbed on her next clutch. Do not clean the aviary, etc. while the birds are incubating and brooding, at least until the young are three weeks old. Birds disturbed too much in the early stages are likely to abandon their eggs or young.

Brooding, Hatching, and Rearing the Young

Most species lay two to five eggs, one every other day. The hen starts to incubate after the last egg has been laid. Incubation time varies, depending on the temperature, but is usually 25 to 26 days. The young leave the nest after about 50 days, but this also depends on the outside temperature.

Newly hatched young have a sparse covering of down. At 15 days the eyes open; at 18 days the first wing feathers break through, and the tail feathers two or three days later. Head and body feathers appear about a week later.

After 20 to 22 days, the young are no longer brooded by the hen. This is all right in the summer (providing the weather is warm) but during spring, late summer, fall, or winter this can be a danger. Young birds that are too cold refuse to feed, quickly lose heat, and die. Some form of heating must thus be provided. For example, you can place an infrared lamp about 28 to 31 inches (70–80 cm) above or alongside the nestbox; by holding your hand in the line of heat, you can determine if it is too hot for your birds.

Pyrrhura Species

In the wild local *Pyrrhura* species have different breeding seasons, especially those inhabiting the Amazon basin, which can breed at any time of the year. Weather conditions and availability of food are two factors that influence the urge to

Breeding South American Conures

breed. These birds are quite social. Two pairs may sometimes nest together in the same nest hole (usually a dark, not-too-deep, hollow limb) or the birds may breed in colonies with nests quite close to each other. After the breeding season the adults and their young forage in groups and spend the night together in or near the old nest. Most *Pyrrhura* species are sexually mature at three years of age and quickly begin to lose their potency in their ninth year.

Housing and Nest Boxes

Pyrrhura species are not too fussy about nest boxes. My rule of thumb about the inner dimensions of the nest boxes is that they should be three-quarters of the body length of the particular species. Thus a bird 9½ inches (24 cm) long (for example, the crimson-bellied conure) requires a box with internal dimensions of 7 x 7 inches (18 x 18 cm). I do not use smaller boxes, although some *Pyrrhura* species will nest in very small ones. Some hens lay large clutches—sometimes seven eggs, of which five will hatch, and the hatchlings will sit with their mother like sardines in a can! Therefore, I always like to give the birds more elbow room.

The floor of the box should be covered with a 1¼-inch (3-cm) layer of woodland soil (which is not tainted with insecticides) mixed with washed aquarium sand and pine bedding. This bedding is used as an absorbent character, since the hen has the strange habit of covering the droppings of the young with material from the nest floor or scrapings from the inside of the box. Thus with four to five young in the nest, the place on which they rest will gradually be raised. To accommodate this, the inspection door in the box should be at least 6 inches (15 cm) above the floor of the nursery.

Because of the hens' gnawing habit, it is best to use natural nesting logs, which have relatively more material to scrape. If, after the first or (if you are lucky) second brood, the nest box is totally destroyed or damaged to the extent that you can see the hen incubating, you must replace it. Try to replace it with a box very similar to the original and put it precisely in the same spot.

The nest boxes should be placed in dark, secluded spots, preferably in the night shelter, against a solid wall. If you hang nest boxes on a wire, fix a wide, solid plank behind them. This gives the birds a more secure feeling.

Brooding, Hatching, and Rearing the Young

The hen begins to incubate sometime after the first (but usually after the third or fourth) egg is laid. The cock brings her food and spends a lot of time in the nest. The hen leaves the nest only to pass her droppings. The normal incubation time for *Pyrrhura* species is 22 to 23 days, depending on the temperature and humidity; in cold, dry weather it can take a few days longer.

The newly hatched young are rosy pink and are covered with a hint of down. The first feathers start to appear after about nine days, and, after 13 days, the eyes begin to open. The white beak begins to take on a grayish pigment (the beak of adults is black). After about 40 days, the young are almost wholly feathered. At first they are fed by the mother; the cock begins to help as they approach fledging time and after they leave the nest. After fledging, the parents continue to feed them for three to four weeks, but I have seen young birds feeding themselves at the food dish after seven to ten days.

As soon as the adults show signs of wanting to start another brood, you should remove the young from the aviary and place them in their own roomy cage or flight, otherwise there is a danger that the adults will get a bit "heavy-handed" with them. Give the young a nest box similar to that in which they were reared (as a sleeping box).

I have had success in placing the young—about three days before they are ready to fledge—in a new but similar nest box next to the old one. The

Breeding South American Conures

adults may seem a little confused at first, but as soon as they hear the young begging for food, they will feed them as usual. The young birds will accept this new box as their sleeping box after they fledge, and it can be moved with them to new quarters when the time is ripe.

When the young are sexually mature (at three years of age) they should be given a nest box similar to that in which they were reared. If you buy an unrelated pair, it is recommended that you find out what sort of nest boxes the breeder used and to copy them. I have found that young placed in a new aviary with the "wrong" type of sleeping box will take months before they get used to it and, in the meantime, will use a perch or ledge high up in the night shelter (see page 19).

In order to refrain from exploiting breeding hens, possibly depleting them of calcium, I recommend that they be allowed to rear only two broods (possibly three under optimal conditions of health, weather, etc.) per season. The nest boxes should be cleaned and disinfected between broods; in some cases the boxes are so badly damaged that they will need to be replaced. The adults do not remove droppings from the nest but bury them below wood splinters and nest linings.

A word about inbreeding. Unfortunately, this happens all too often, especially with rare birds where it is difficult to get a compatible, unrelated pair. *Pyrrhura* species are especially vulnerable to this practice, which can have disastrous consequences, leading to nonviable offspring.

Therefore, breed only with unrelated pairs that are healthy and at least three years old.

If you need to replace a partner (perhaps the pair do not get along with each other), place the new bird alone in the aviary for two or three days before introducing the original bird into it. If the birds start to fight, you must separate them again and look for a new partner. If you have several breeding pairs, it is possible to transfer eggs, or youngsters, from one nest to another. For example, if you have one pair with a large number of eggs or young, you can foster some of them to other parents with smaller clutches. But be sure that you do not place newly laid eggs in a nest where the eggs are about to hatch!

Pyrrhura species can be kept in community aviaries with birds of similar size (although I always prefer the rule, "one pair to one aviary"). These birds normally live in colonies and have a rank order not unlike that of domestic fowl. The stronger individuals prevail over the weaker ones. Thus in an aviary you can see the strongest pairs go to nest, while the weaker ones barely get a chance. A very large aviary—with many escape routes and hiding places—that does not contain too many pairs would provide an opportunity for all birds to breed. I have found that each pair needs a minimum of 8 to 10 square feet (2.5–3.0 m²) of floor area.

All birds in the group must be introduced to the aviary at the same time. Never add new pairs to an existing group shortly before, during, or shortly after the breeding season. Each pair must have a choice of at least two nest boxes.

Top: The plain, all-green or tirica parakeet (*Brotogeris* ▶ *tirica*) is well-known in captivity. The species requires a large aviary.
Bottom: Like the tirica, the golden winged parakeet (*B. c. chrysopterus*) requires maggots, white worms, mealworms, and, especially, ant pupae as rearing food—along with safflower, sunflower, canary grass, and millet seed. Various fruits are also appreciated.

South American Conure Species

Genus *Aratinga*

Within the genus *Aratinga* there is a great variety of color and form, from which every fancier will find something to his or her liking. The most beautiful member of the genus is reputed to be the Queen of Bavaria conure, which, with its golden color, is a treat for the eyes. Unfortunately, this is one of the rarest and thus most expensive species. There are a few green to brownish green subspecies that are less attractive, including the white-eyed, the Hispaniolan and Jamaican conures and some brown-throated conures. But these subspecies have their own attractions. There are also considerable variations in total lengths—from the Petz, Jamaican, and some subspecies of the St. Thomas conures, at 9½ inches (24 cm), to the Peruvian conure, at 16½ inches (42 cm). Members of this genus are similar to the macaws; the dwarf macaws are especially similar to the sharp-tailed conure.

All species and subspecies are found in a large area of Central and South America, from Mexico to central Argentina. The genus is also well represented in the islands of the West Indies.

The huge area of distribution of these conures means an immense variety of habitats, ranging from tropical rain forest to savanna, desert to semidesert, montane to sea level. Here, however, unlike in the northern temperate zones, the temperature is relatively constant throughout the year, as are the hours of daylight. Therefore, the birds are not too particular about the timing of the breeding season.

◀ Top: The santarem or taka-tsukasa parakeet (*Brotogeris sanctithomae takatsukasae*) is a subspecies of the well-known tui parakeet (*B. s. sanctithomae*), but is rather rare in captivity. The species however is similar to the nominate form except for a yellow streak behind the eye. The pictured birds were bred by my friend F. Mertens in the Netherlands.

Bottom: The gray-cheeked or orange-flanked parakeet (*B. pyrrhopterus*) is an excellent pet, quiet, affectionate but destructive.

In captivity eggs are often laid from early spring to late summer. In general, however, they are later than Australian parakeets.

The scientific name *Aratinga* derives from the fact that these birds are similar to macaws (genus *Ara*): "tinga" is a diminutive, so that "aratinga" means "little macaw." Most species are fully grown in their third year. It is noteworthy that most of the young at fledging time are greener than the adult green color. In the larger species (recognized by a white beak and flesh-colored feet), the young are wholly green, without a hint of a red feather; these first appear only when they are about three months old.

Experience has shown that pairs dislike being moved. If a particular pair is breeding well in an aviary, it is best left there. If a breeding pair is relocated, you can usually "kiss breeding goodbye" for that particular season! Most species, however, do not seem to mind if you occasionally inspect the eggs or young in the nest. In general, most *Aratinga* species seem to make excellent parents.

Aratinga species are not particularly fussy when it comes to choosing nest sites. Natural logs or artificial nest boxes are accepted. *A. pertinax* and *A. cactorum* breed in rock crevices in the wild, but will accept a nest box with a long entrance tunnel (see illustration on page 38)

Cocks and hens are outwardly very similar in appearance, although I believe that hens possess a grayer iris than cocks. But you can make such decisions only when you have adequate comparative material. According to some aviculturists, the hens also have a somewhat coarser head. My friend, the late Mrs. J. Spenkelink van Schaik told me that *Aratinga* species have sexual differences similar to those of macaws: in cocks the feathers on the edge of the forehead and between the nostrils and eyes are longer and wider than in the hens, giving the effect of eyebrows. Also, in cocks, the curve of the beak is stronger than in the hens, giving the appearance of a "hump" on the upper beak.

South American Conure Species

Aratinga species should not be kept in too dry or too warm accommodations, otherwise they are likely to pluck their feathers. Fresh air, sunshine, and a daily bath will keep members of this genus in top condition.

If one of the partners of a breeding pair dies, this can create some problems. The remaining bird often pines to death. The larger the species, the greater the problem may be. According to Mrs. J. Spenkelink van Schaik, if a Queen of Bavaria cock should lose his mate, he is unlikely to accept another. "In order to reduce the chance of him pining away," she wrote me, " I had young *Aratinga* species, such as *A. leucophthalmus, A. wagleri, A. rubritorquis* and *A. auricapilla* in the colony. The following experience proved that I had made the right decision: The hen of my pair of Queen of Bavaria conures (which seemed to have settled well into their nest box) suddenly died. The cock could do nothing but roll the body of the hen around. The following day, long after the hen's body had been removed, he stayed in the nest box rummaging and digging. When he collected food, he took it to the nest box and made feeding movements at the entrance as though the hen was still there. The following day, I placed all my non-breeding *Aratinga* species with the cock Queen of Bavaria in another aviary. After a few days I saw a little improvement in his behavior and fourteen days later he was going into a nest box with a Golden-capped conure. He got over the loss of his 'wife' in about three weeks."

"When I had, at last, obtained another hen Queen of Bavaria conure, I placed the pair together in a new aviary. After a few initial difficulties, he eventually accepted his new hen."

Sharp-tailed Conure
(*A. acuticaudata acuticaudata*)

The sharp-tailed conure has a blue forehead, crown, and cheeks; it has a blue stripe from the beak to the eye and is blue around the ears. The blue color in this species covers a greater area than in the other subspecies. I have even seen examples with blue on the breast. The underside of the wings is yellowish olive. The underside of the tail is olive green and reddish at the base of most feathers. The upper mandible is dark brown with a darker tip; the lower mandible is blackish. The eye ring is white and conspicuous. The iris is yellow, and the feet are brownish pink. Length: 14⅗ inches (37 cm). Weight: 6.7 ounces (190 g).

The nominate form inhabits the relatively dry regions of eastern Brazil, southwestern Mato Grosso, Paraguay, Uruguay, and northern Argentina. The birds live in small groups. They are noisy and can cause damage to crops and plantations.

This species is regularly bred in captivity. The young—as with most *Aratinga* species—are difficult to distinguish from the adults once they are fully feathered, except for the horn-colored beak and somewhat lighter eye ring.

The nominate form was probably bred for the first time in captivity by the Englishman K. Bastien on the Isle of Wight in 1971. The captive-bred young quickly became tame and affectionate and were extremely intelligent but, unfortunately, had very loud voices! It was remarkable that some of the young possessed red feathers on the shoulders and wings, something that did not occur in the parents.

In 1987 I obtained a number of sexed pairs. Five pairs became sexually mature after two years; two pairs reached maturity after two-and-a-half years. Each pair has its own flight, 19 feet (6 m) long, and a choice of three nest boxes, 7.9 inches (20 cm) long, 19½ inches (50 cm) deep, and 7.9 inches (20 cm) high, with an entrance hole 3.2 inches (8 cm) in diameter.

The hens average three eggs per clutch. The hen incubates the eggs alone for an average of 24 days. After 45 days the young are fully feathered, and they leave the nest after 58 days. After laying the first egg, the hen seldom leaves the nest and is fed by the cock.

South American Conure Species

Major Differences Between Various Green Conures (*Aratinga*)							
	Length (inches)	Forehead	Crown	Band of Wing	Thigh	Small Underwing Coverts	Underwing Coverts
A. h. holochlora Mexican Green Conure	12½	Green	Green	Green	Green	Yellowish Green	Yellowish Green
A. finschi Finsch's Conure	11	Red	Green	Red	Red	Red	Yellow
A. w. wagleri Wagler's Conure	14⅕	Red	Red	Green	Green	Green	Olive Green
A. m. mitrata Mitered Conure	15	Red	Green	Green	Green	Olive Green	Olive Green
A. erythrogenys Red-masked Conure	13	Red	Red	Red	Red	Red	Olive-yellow
A. l. leucophthalmus White-eyed Conure	12½	Green	Green	Red	Red	Red	Gold-yellow
A. c. chloroptera Hispaniolan Conure	12½	Green	Green	Red	Green	Green	Red
A. euops Cuban Conure	10¼	Green	Green	Red	Green	Red	Olive-yellow

This species is somewhat noisy, though not as bad as the Jenday conures, sun conures or Nanday conures. When the birds have eggs or young, they are very quiet. In general, all my birds are reasonably peaceful.

Blue-crowned Conure
(A. a. haemorrhous)

The color of this subspecies is similar to the nominate form *(A. a. acuticaudata)*, with less blue (pale blue only on the forehead and front part of crown). The green is a more intensive shade, and both upper and lower mandibles are horn colored. Length: 13¾ inches (35 cm). Weight: 6.8 ounces (193 g).

The species ranges from northern Venezuela (including Margarita islands), through eastern Colombia, to southwestern Mato Grosso and eastern Brazil, including Piauy and northern Bahia.

This species, which is difficult to distinguish from the nominate form, is commonly seen in cages and aviaries (despite its export ban from Brazil, Colombia, and Venezuela). Although the birds have loud and raucous voices, they become very affectionate toward their handler, are intelligent, and make ideal pets. A good pair will breed readily if given the right conditions.

Both this and the foregoing subspecies are tolerant in a community aviary, though they may become somewhat aggressive during the breeding season. Both subspecies are shy, so that they are likely to become hand tame only in a sturdy cage or small aviary, where they can take tidbits from the hand; in roomy aviaries they will tend to fly away. In general, their loud voices are tolerable and likely to grate only if the birds are shocked or excited. But I would recommend that you discuss matters with your neighbors before you obtain such noisy birds.

Good breeding results can be obtained using a nest box with an entrance porch (see figure on page 38) measuring 19½ x 9.8 x 9.8 inches (50 x 25 x 25 cm).

South American Conure Species

Mexican Green Conure
(A. holochlora holochlora)

The main color of these birds is green (yellowish green on the belly). Sometimes there are a few red feathers on the head, throat and neck; these are more common in cocks than in hens. There is some black on the wings, pale yellowish green below the tail. The beak is flesh colored, and the wide eye rings are light pink. The iris is orange-red. Length: 12.6 inches (32 cm). Weight: 6.3 ounces (179 g).

The species is found in eastern and southern Mexico, from Nuevo Leon to Veracruz, Oaxaca, and Chiapas. Within their range the birds generally live in montane regions or in the foothills, where their gnawing tendencies can cause much agricultural damage, especially to pine plantations. They live in noisy social groups of 26 to 38 birds. Males and females form a very strong pair bond, usually for life.

Members of this species are readily available. The first successful breeding results probably were obtained in the United States in 1934, but reported breedings have always been scarce. The birds are best kept in small groups of three to four pairs. They must have a rich choice of seeds (including soaked) as well as tree leaves, fresh fruit, and dandelion leaves.

Socorro Green Conure
(A. h. brevipes)

The main color of this subspecies is dark green, especially on the head. The underside is also dark green, without the yellow sheen. There are never any red feathers on the throat or neck. According to Thomas Arndt, the tenth primary flight feather is shorter than the seventh, which is the opposite of all other subspecies. Length: about 12.6 inches (32 cm).

This subspecies occurs only on the island of Socorro in the Pacific Ocean, about 375 miles (600 km) off the west coast of Mexico. Here, the birds live in the montane forests.

Brewster's Green Conure
(A. h. brewsteri)

This subspecies is similar in color to the preceding subspecies, but is even darker, with a little blue on the crown. Length: to about 12½ inches (32 cm). Weight: 4.7 ounces (133 g).

The subspecies is found in northwestern Mexico (Sonora, Sinaloa and Chihuahua), living high in the mountains, often at altitudes of 6,000 feet (2,600 m).

Nicaraguan Green Conure
(A. h. strenua)

This conure subspecies is similar in color to *A. h. holochlora*, but is longer (13⅓ inches or 34 cm), with a more robust beak. Weight: 5.1 ounces (145 g).

The Nicaraguan green conure *(Aratinga holochlora strenua)* is scarce in the lowland areas but occurs frequently in agricultural regions.

South American Conure Species

The birds inhabit the hilly coast of Mexico to northern Nicaragua. They are frequently found in agricultural regions, where they can cause much damage.

All *holochlora* subspecies are found mainly in coniferous woodlands, sometimes high in the mountains. They are noisy birds and can easily be heard even when they fly quite high in the sky. They have a fast, elegant, and very economical flight pattern. In the wild they use old woodpecker holes, termite hills, or rock crevices as nesting sites. They usually breed in the early months of the year, but also in August to December in Guatemala and until April in Mexico.

Red-throated or Red-collared Conure
(A. h. rubritorquis)

The main color is green with orange-red on the throat, sometimes reaching to the upper breast.

The red-throated conure *(Aratinga holochlora rubri-tor-quis)* is known to tolerate rather low temperatures.

Sometimes there are red feathers near the lower mandible and on the neck. Otherwise the subspecies is similar to *A. h. holochlora*. It grows to a length of 11.8 inches (30 cm). Weight: 4.2 ounces (119 g).

The species ranges from eastern Guatemala, through Honduras, to northern Nicaragua. Birds of this species are rarely seen in aviculture, but specimens can be seen at the bird park at Walsrode in Germany.

Mr. J. De Ruyt of the Netherlands bred three young successfully. There were four eggs in the clutch, which hatched in 24 to 25 days. The eyes of the young opened on the 12th day. The first hatchling fledged at 54 days. At 36 weeks of age the birds were sexed and found to be two cocks and a hen. It is interesting to note that the parent pair had been together in the aviary for six years before going to nest!

Finsch's Conure
(A. h. finschi)

The forehead is scarlet, which sometimes runs through to the eyes. This red may also be found among the green and yellow under the wings. The wing joint is also red, and the iris is orange. The birds reach a length of 11 inches (28 cm). Weight: 5.5 to 6.3 ounces (156–179 g).

The species is native to Central America, from Nicaragua to western Panama, but is absent from western Costa Rica. These are extremely active birds. They are quite abundant in the wild, especially in agricultural areas. They seem to prefer cultivated areas interspersed with natural woodland, but inhabit only the woodland edges. They like to rest in low vegetation. The species is frequently seen in the Caribbean lowlands, often in groups of 10 to 100 birds, but it may also be seen in the mountains. The birds seem to pair up for life.

Like some parrots, these birds frequently hang upside down from a twig, often using only one foot—and making a comical sight as well as show-

South American Conure Species

The Finsch's conure *(Aratinga holochlora finschi)* is lively and noisy in captivity as well as in the wild, although it becomes silent at dusk and, it seems, during heavy rainfall.

ing their acrobatic abilities. The groups feed, drink, and sleep together. I have studied these birds in the wild in their roosting areas. Sometimes there were over 300 birds present, making an ear-shattering noise in their squabbles over the best roosting sites. They feed on seeds, fruit, berries, nuts and green food. They will sometimes eat wheat, corn, or other grain, but only when other food supplies are insufficient.

In the bird park at Walsrode, Germany, these birds have bred in a nest log 23⅔ inches (60 cm) deep and 7.9 inches (20 cm) in diameter, with an entrance hole 3.5 inches (9 cm) in diameter placed 11.8 inches (30 cm) above the floor of the log. The log was barely gnawed at by the birds. They would probably also accept a nest box 15¾ to 19½ inches (40–50 cm) high with a floor area of 7.9 x 7.9 inches (20 x 20 cm). A 2¾-inch (7-cm) entrance hole would seem to be adequate.

Little is known about the wild breeding habits of this species; we have only the breeding report from Walsrode. In 1982 one bird was hatched, but the parents refused to feed it and it could not be saved. In 1988 four eggs were laid in early June, and the hen started to incubate after the second egg. The cock stayed close to the nest log and joined the hen at night. The first two young hatched after 23 days, the third a day later. The fourth egg was infertile. The young fledged in 56, 56, and 57 days, respectively. They had no red in their plumage, and the forehead was darker in color.

Wagler's Conure *(A. wagleri wagleri)*

The forehead and crown are a variation of red. There is a red band (or spots) on the throat. The rest of the body is green—olive green beneath the wings and tail, and a lighter green on the underside and on the back. There are a few red feathers on the cheeks, neck, and thighs. The beak is light horn colored, and the wide eye ring is beige-white. The iris is orange and the feet are brownish. Length: 14⅕ inches (36 cm). Weight: 6.4 ounces (181 g). Young birds show no red on the head or throat, but they are similar to the adults as soon as they come through the first molt.

This species is found in the maritime regions of Colombia, into the Cauca and Magdalana valleys and the area of Santa Marter. It also extends northward alongh the coast of Venezuela. It is found at an altitude of 2,625 to 6,500 feet (800–2,000 m) in the subtropical woodlands.

In the wild the birds breed in colonies, in rock crevices, often on high and inaccessible cliff faces. Colonies have been known to use the same sites for 25 years or more. Outside the breeding season the birds assemble in groups of about 300 and travel around in search of food and roosting sites. They are extremely quarrelsome, especially when going to roost at night.

The nominate species was first bred in the United States in 1957, followed by Germany in 1978. In 1969, the Chester zoo, in England, exhibited a colony of these birds, and in 1978 it had the third generation of young in the aviary. Breeding results with the other subspecies are poorly documented, although they should not be discounted.

South American Conure Species

The birds are occasionally imported and can be seen at Walsrode in Germany and at the Antwerp zoo in Belgium. It is possible to cross this species with the Jenday conure, although the breeding of hybrids is now frowned upon. The birds feed on a variety of leaves, flowers, twigs of willow and fruit trees, and a great variety of grass and weed seeds (as well as the usual parakeet seed mixture).

The birds make excellent pets and will thrive in a roomy cage in the house. They become tame and affectionate in a relatively short time. They are extremely intelligent and can soon learn all kinds of tricks. Wild birds often have an ear-piercing screech, but birds bred in captivity seldom use their voices in this manner.

It is difficult to imitate the natural nesting sites of these birds in captivity. However, they will frequently accept a nest box or log 19½ inches (50 cm) high and with a floor area of 7.9 x 7.9 inches (20 x 20 cm). The entrance hole should not exceed 2¾ inches (7 cm). Inventive fanciers can, of course, experiment with artificial "rock faces" with crevices; this could be done with concrete. One should ensure that these crevices cannot be flooded with rainwater. Such a construction is not only good for the birds, but puts a new face on our sometimes monotonous aviaries.

Mitered Conure (*A. mitrata mitrata*)

Adults of this species have an irregular red pattern on the head. The most distinctive feature is the red color around the eye. Except for the red-masked conure, the mitered conure has the greatest amount of red on the head. It also has red feathers sprinkled irregularly all over the body. After each molt, these feathers do not necessary reappear in the same place. The iris is orange-yellow. The subspecies *A. m. alticola* has less red on the head; it is limited to a narrow forehead band. In addition, the green of the plumage shows a bluish tint. It is about ⅓ inch (1 cm) shorter than the nominate species which is about 15 inches (38 cm) in total length. Weight: 8.6 ounces (244 g). Young birds sometimes show a sprinkling of red feathers, but in smaller quantity. Moreover, they have less red on the head; this is limited to a broad forehead band. The eyes and the feet are noticeably darker in color in the young than in the adults.

This species is replacing Wagler's conure in the Andes of central and southern Peru (where the ranges of the two species overlap), and along the eastern slopes of Bolivia to northwestern Argentina. The two species are very closely related. The subspecies, called Chapman's mitered conure, has a limited range around Cuzco, Peru, at an altitude of 11,150 feet (3,400 m). It is a montane species, though the nominate form may be encountered to an altitude of 8,000 feet (2,500 m), and spends its nights in large groups in the rain forest.

There is only one example of nesting behavior in the wild. This nest was found in a hollow tree at a height of about 30 feet (10 m). There were two eggs in it. The hollow was quite large, and the entrance hole was wide.

An English fancier reported successful breeding in a cubic nest box measuring 11.8 x 11.8 x 11.8 inches (30 x 30 x 30 cm). But it is better to use a box 15¾ to 19½ inches (40–50 cm) deep with a floor area of 6.0 to 7.9 square inches (15–20 cm²) or a hollow log with an inner diameter of 7.9 inches (20 cm). The entrance hole should be 2¾ to 3⅕ inches (7–8 cm) in diameter.

A pair of birds was bred in captivity in Germany in 1982. Three eggs, each weighing 1 ounce (14 g) and measuring 28 by 34 millimeters, were laid. The hen started to incubate as soon as the first egg was laid, and the incubation time was about 26 days (this is not certain, however, since only one of the eggs hatched, and it is not known if it was the first one). The young bird, weighing 8 ounces (220 g), left the nest at 59 days.

A German fancier bred the species in 1984. Eggs were laid on the 5th, 7th and 9th of May, but, although they were fertile, they did not hatch. A second clutch was laid on the 25th, 27th, and 29th June. The hen started to incubate after the first egg had been laid. The eggs hatched on 18th, 20th, and 22nd of July (thus the incubation time was 23 days). The young left the nest on the 66th day. They had just a red forehead band.

An English fancier hatched eggs in an incubator. These measured 26.2 by 32.5 millimeters. The newly hatched young weighed 0.289 and 0.293 ounces (8.27 and 8.38 g). The eyes opened after about two weeks, and the birds were leg banded at 23 days. They had red feathers here and there on the head. They were independent after nine weeks.

The birds bathe frequently in the aviary. In general, they remain shy for a relatively long time. They are very hardy and can withstand quite low temperatures. Although they are not totally unknown in aviculture, they are not frequently available.

Red-masked or Red-headed Conure (*A. erythrogenys*)

With the exception of the rear half of the cheeks, the head is wholly red. There are frequently red feathers on the throat and neck as well as the shoulders, the underside of the wings, the wing joint, and thigh feathers. The primaries are yellowish green beneath, as is the underside of the tail. The iris is yellow-orange, the beak horn colored, and the feet dark gray. Length: 13 inches (33 cm). Weight: male, 6.5 ounces (184 g); hen, 5.8 ounces (164 g). The young have a little red only on the wings, though I have had a few young that had red feathers on the head at five months.

Formerly known also as *A. rubrolarvatus*, this species occurs in southwestern Ecuador and northwestern Peru.

This is a very abundant species that is also found in aviculture. Unfortunately, the birds have a nerve-grating call, and even hand-tame specimens retain this habit, though they can learn to repeat a few words.

Regular breeding successes have been reported. The hen lays three to four eggs (31.1 by 26.6 millimeters); incubation time is about 25 days. The young leave the nest after about six weeks. A nest box 11 x 10½ inches (28 x 27 cm) with a depth of 21¼ inches (54 cm) and an entrance hole 4⅓ inches (11 cm) in diameter is ideal for this species.

White-eyed Conure or Green Conure (*A. leucophthalmus leucophthalmus*)

This species is green with red feathers on the head, throat, and neck. The wing coverts are red, and there is some red below the wings. The first primaries are yellowish green. The underside of the tail is beige to golden yellow. The heavy beak is light horn colored. Length: about 13⅓ inches (34 cm). Weight: 4.6 ounces (130 g). Young specimens have a yellow wing bend.

White-eyed conures range from Venezuela and Guyana, southward through Brazil and eastern Bolivia to Argentina, Paraguay, and Uruguay. They live in pairs or small groups throughout the year.

Although they are rarely available, irregular breeding successes have been reported. The hen lays three to four—sometimes five—eggs. The young leave the nest after about 65 days.

These birds are shy, taking a long time to become accustomed to their keeper. They shriek in alarm at the slightest disturbance. They have a rather unfortunate tendency to eat too many sunflower seeds and ignore other food. Persuade them to eat other seeds such as hemp, millet, and canary grass seed, as well as apples, pears, and pieces of banana.

Cuba Conure (*A. euops*)

The Cuba conure is green with some red feathers on the head and neck, the thighs, and—in some cases—on the flanks. It has red wing coverts, a light flesh-colored beak, and a white eye ring. Length: 10½ inches (26.5 cm). Weight: 3.5 ounces (99 g).

The species occurs on the island of Cuba; at one time it was also found on the Isle of Pines, but it seems to have disappeared from there. At the beginning of this century these birds were extremely abundant in Cuba, in the woods and sometimes in the open country, where they did damage to crops. During the last few decades the population has decreased dramatically, to near extinction. This is probably due to loss of habitat through human action. In order to clear land for agriculture, breeding sites such as hollow trees and woodpecker holes have been totally destroyed, leaving the birds nowhere to reproduce.

These birds were rarely common or easily available in aviculture. From the literature we can surmise that they were active, noisy, argumentative, and destructive birds not very tolerant toward other species.

The German, S. Fuss (Rottenburg), has had a pair of these birds in his possession since the late 1970s, and these have been producing young since 1986.

The birds feed on seeds (especially fond of sunflower seeds), nuts, buds, berries, and fruit. The hen lays three to five white eggs, which are incubated by both sexes for 23 days. The young leave the nest after about 45 days.

Golden-headed or Golden-capped Conure *(A. auricapilla auricapilla)*

The main color is dark green with the front of the crown yellow or brown-red (see Jenday conure); the back of head and neck light yellowish green. The sides of the head are green with a yellow tinge. There is a little yellow or brown-red around the eyes and ears, and a broad yellow crown. The throat and upper breast are green. The upper belly has brownish red blotches with green (green base to feathers only). Length: 11⅘ inches (30 cm). Weight: 5.3 ounces (150 g). The young have a deeper color, with more brownish red on the flanks and lower belly. They are sexually mature at two years of age.

This species is native to southeastern Brazil

The golden-headed conure *(Aratinga auricapilla auricapilla)* is an extremely popular pet bird in the United States.

(Bahia). It is a very popular cage and aviary bird in the United States. It is quite easy to breed in a roomy aviary. The bird is sometimes confused with the Jenday conure and requires similar care.

One subspecies is the golden-fronted conure *(A. a. aurifrons)* from southeastern Brazil (Minas Geraës, Rio de Janeiro, São Paolo and Paraná). This bird has a somewhat larger head. The wide orange-red band extends to the crown. The rump feathers are green (these have a reddish brown border in the nominate form).

The golden-headed conure is a hardy bird and can tolerate our climates well even in the winter in an outdoor aviary, provided that it has adequate shelter from the elements. A young hen usually lays just two eggs, but clutches get bigger as she ages. Best breeding results have usually occurred in deep nest boxes (41 x 9 x 6⅓ inches, or 103 x 23 x 16 cm). The hen lays three to five eggs, which hatch in 25 days.

Jenday Conure
(A. (auricapillus) jandaya)

The head, neck, and upper part of the breast are golden yellow, merging into deep reddish-gold on the rest of the lower body. The thigh feathers are olive green, frequently sprinkled with small red feathers. Sometimes olive-yellow feathers are found on the breast. Most of the back, the wings, and rump are all green; the lowest part of the back is orange-red. Wing feathers are blue, as is the tip of the tail. The base of the tail is metallic brownish-green and the underside is black. The beak is also black. Some specimens have white and others black eye rings, which could indicate separate subspecies. The length is 11⅕ inches (30 cm). Weight: male, 4.4 ounces (125 g); hen, 5.0 ounces (142 g). The young have pale citron-yellow feathers with green edges. They become sexually mature at two years of age.

Jenday conures are native to northeastern Brazil (Maranhão, Piauhy to northern Goliás and Ceará). They live in small groups in thick, thorny bush country in the Brazilian mountains. They are sometimes seen in more open areas that were once covered with rain forest.

These brilliant but often noisy birds are probably the best known members of the genus *Aratinga*. They are bred frequently and successfully and appear to be, along with the sun conures, which follow, the most popular and commonly kept and bred conures in the United States. It is possible to breed hybrids with the Nanday conure, but this is not recommended. The hen incubates three to four eggs, and these hatch after about 26 days. Both parents feed the young after they hatch. The young leave the nest at about two months of age but are fed by the parents for about a week longer.

A nest box measuring 21⅔ x 9⅘ x 11 inches (55 x 25 x 28 cm) is ideal. The entrance hole should

The sun conure (*Aratinga (auricapilla) solstitialis*) may be seen in small or large groups to an altitude of 4,000 feet (1,200 m).

be about 2¾ inches (7 cm) in diameter, though the birds may alter this to their liking.

Sun Conure
(A. (auricapillus) solstitialis)

This species is similar in color to the Jenday conure, but it is yellower and has more gold-orange tints (which frequently glint orange), especially below the wings and sometimes in a fairly large area around the eyes. The wings are green with yellow tips. The large primaries are dark blue; the small primaries have green borders. The shoulder feathers are yellow. The tail is a dull yellow-green, frequently with a blue tip. The beak is blackish-blue, and the eye ring is white. Length: 11⅕ inches (30 cm). Weight: 4.6 ounces (130 g). Juveniles are mainly light green, with a lot of yellow appearing at about four months of age. The wings and tail are yellowish below and dark blue at the end. The crown and back of the head are orange-yellow with green tints. The iris is pale brown. The full adult plumage is complete at about 18 months, and the birds are sexually mature at two years.

Sun conures occur naturally in Guyana, northwestern Brazil, and Surinam. They may be seen in small or large groups on the southern savannas or in open and light woodlands to an altitude of 4,000 feet (1,200 m).

This spectacular species is seldom seen in captivity. In the past, however, breeding success has been achieved frequently, especially with single pairs in roomy aviaries. A German fancier gave a pair a choice of one nest box measuring 17¾ x 11⅘ x 11⅘ inches (45 x 30 x 30 cm) and a natural log with a 15¾-inch (40-cm) diameter and a height of 32 inches (80 cm). The first was preferred, until the natural log was replaced by another 47 inches (120 cm) high and with a diameter of 17¾ inches (45 cm). This was used to rear a family.

This species is infamous for its loud, nerve-grating voice, but it is not difficult to breed. The incubation time is 24 days; the newly hatched young are covered with grayish-white down. Corn on the cob and various ears of grain can be given as extra rearing food, as well as grass seeds, fruit, green food, whole meal bread, bread soaked in milk and squeezed out, hard-boiled egg, boiled rice, oats, dried shrimp, mealworms, and canary rearing food. During winter the birds should be kept in a lightly heated shelter to avoid frostbite of the toes.

Queen of Bavaria Conure
(A. guarouba)

Adult, fully feathered birds are a brilliant golden yellow; only the primaries and secondaries are green. The beak is pale horn colored (frequently larger in the cock than the hen). They have a relatively short tail, a narrow, naked, white eye ring, brown to black iris, and light pink feet. Length: about 14 inches (35.5 cm). Weight: 8.8 ounces (249 g). Juvenile birds have green feathers in the

plumage, and the yellow is duller. At 18 months they are usually fully feathered.

Queen of Bavaria conures are native to northeastern Brazil, south of the Amazon from the Rio Xingu to Maranhão, probably also Ceará (according to Rosemary Low). This species is protected, since it has become extremely rare in the wild. Nothing much is known about its natural habits. The clearing of thousands of acres of jungle, the building of dams, and the construction of highways have drastically reduced the natural habitat of this species. While groups of 6 to 30 birds could be seen a few years ago, one is now lucky to see two or three.

The first breeding results date from 1939 in Sri Lanka. In 1940 young were born in Liverpool, England, and in the United States in 1945. Regular successes have been reported since then.

The hen lays three to four eggs (24 by 34 millimeters). The incubation period is about 25 days, and the young stay in the nest for about 10

The Queen of Bavaria conure (*Aratinga guarouba*). As they come into breeding condition, these birds become particularly aggressive and can even attack their owner.

weeks before fledging. The main feathers on the wings and tail appear at 35 days, and the young are fully feathered at six weeks. The parents continue to feed the young after they leave the nest, though they can usually feed themselves after four to five days. The young clamber over the perches and the aviary wire for some time, rather than use their wings. Fresh corn on the cob, germinated seeds, fruit, and adequate drinking water are important for satisfactory development of the young.

Although I usually give measurements for nest boxes, queen of Bavaria conures are not particularly fussy when it comes to finding a place to rear a family. It should not be too small, however, and the floor should be covered with a layer of wood pulp and sand. In most cases the birds will first use this as sleeping quarters, then to rear their young when the breeding season arrives. The box should be made of tough hardwood, since these birds are very destructive.

These expensive birds are tame and affectionate toward their owner. They are intelligent and always lively in the cage or aviary. The only disadvantage is their loud, nerve-splitting call. They often are aggressive toward each other and other species, even toward much larger birds. They will even visit the nests of other psittacines and pluck the feathers from the nestlings! During the breeding season these birds become particularly aggressive and can even attack their owner.

Another bad habit of these birds is that of feather plucking. The reason for this is not known. The limited space in the aviary may offer insufficient amusement, bringing on boredom and exaggerated feather care. Plenty of things to occupy the birds (including regular food changes) and freedom of movement can help avoid this bad habit. Nutritional supplements such as protein, calcium, and other minerals (always necessary for feather growth) are important. But steroids, tranquilizers, and/or hormones prescribed by a veterinarian may also be required. It is recommended that feather pluckers be examined by an avian veterinarian.

The dusky-headed conure *(Aratinga weddelli)* is a hardy bird and can spend the winter outdoors if a proper night shelter is provided.

Dusky-headed or Weddell's Conure *(A. weddelli)*

This species is mainly green. The head has a grayish-blue sheen. The naked eye ring is white. The blue tint varies with the amount of light, appearing deeper in sunlight than in artificial light. There is a yellowish green sheen on the belly, and the ends of the primaries and tail feathers are blue. Newly fledged youngsters have a duller color, and the belly is green. The birds are sexually mature at two years of age. Length: 11 inches (28 cm). Weight: 4.1 ounces (116 g).

Weddell's conure occurs naturally along watercourses in the Amazon basin and in tropical woodlands on the eastern edge of the Andes in Colombia. The birds frequent the woods and savannas of the lowlands in groups of about 20 individuals.

This relatively quiet and peaceful conure is not well known in avicultural circles. It starts to breed early in the year. The hen lays three to four eggs, which are incubated for about 24 days. The young leave the nest about 55 days later. To stimulate the breeding urge of the hen, a few pieces of half-rotten wood should be placed in the nest box. She will immediately begin to chew these up. Many breeders have reported that these birds take only egg food (such as L/M Universal-Plus or CéDé) when they have young in the nest.

In general, this is a hardy species that can spend the winter outdoors if a damp and draftproof shelter is provided. It has been reported that a breeder in Rio de Janeiro was blessed with a yellow mutation of this species.

Petz' or Orange-fronted Conure
(A. canicularis canicularis)

This bird is similar in appearance to the peach-fronted conure but is easy to differentiate by its macaw-like beak. The upper mandible is horn colored; the lower is horn colored and black on the sides. The plumage is green, with greenish-yellow on the lower parts. The underside of the wings and tail is yellow. The forehead is orange; the crown is partly orange with blue. The primaries are blue, thinly edged in green. The eye ring is naked and orange-yellow (in the peach-fronted conure small orange feathers are present here). Juveniles possess less orange color than the adults; they have a brown iris and a narrower orange forehead band. Length: 9½ inches (24 cm). Weight: male, 2.7 ounces (77 g); hen, 2.5 ounces (71 g).

This species is native to Central America, from the Isthmus of Tehauntepec southward to western Costa Rica. The birds sometimes live in quite large groups, especially in the northwestern part of their habitat, in bush land and sparsely treed, open savanna.

Petz' conure is one of the most abundant parakeets in United States aviculture. It is almost as popular as the canary or budgerigar and so common as to be available quite cheaply for most of the year. Many people keep it as a cage pet, and it seems to do very well. It becomes especially tame

The Petz' conure *(Aratinga c. canicularis)* is extremely popular, especially as it soon becomes finger-tame and can learn to speak a few words.

and affectionate and can learn to speak a few words. Since little seems to have been done to promote captive breeding of this species, reports of successes are not common.

In Walsrode, Germany, the southern Mexican subspecies bred in 1988 in the parrot house. The pair shared a 7 x 10 x 9.9-inch (2.2 x 3 x 2.1-m) aviary with a pair of Leadbeater's cockatoos! Each of the three eggs were laid at two day intervals. Incubation started with the first egg, and the time taken was 23 days. The young left the nest after 49 days. They were quite similar to the adults, but the orange forehead band was narrower and the iris was darker. They stayed with their parents for more than six months.

In the wild the birds breed in termite mounds (of the species *Nasutitermes nigriceps*), where they dig out a tunnel and chamber with their beaks. The entrance has a diameter of about 2¾ inches (7 cm).

The tunnel slopes upward for about 11¾ inches (30 cm), and the nest chamber is 6 to 8 inches (15–20 cm) in diameter. The whole construction takes about a week, and then a week of rest is taken (probably to allow the termites to repair their tunnels). Sometimes, abandoned woodpeckers' nests are used.

Although the birds have been known to use artificial nest boxes, better results would probably be obtained if some attempt were made to provide captive birds with the kind of nesting they would find in nature. In Walsrode successful breeding took place in a box 24 inches (60 cm) high and 11¾ inches (30 cm) in diameter, with an entrance "tunnel" 11¾ inches (30 cm) long.

Half-Moon Conure
(*A. c. eburnirostrum*)

This subspecies is similar in color to the Petz, but a little larger. The lower mandible is

The half-moon conure *(Aratinga canicularis eburnirostrum)* frequents leafless trees as "look-outs." It is interesting to see the trees full of motionless birds, even while a bird of prey is capturing one of them!

gray-brown, and the flanks are less yellow-green. Length: about 9½ inches (24 cm). Weight: 2.6 ounces (74 g).

These birds are native to southwestern Mexico (Sinaloa, Durango, Nayarit, Colima, and Gueriero). They usually live in lively, alert, and noisy groups. They have special "lookout" trees, from where they can keep watch on what's going on around them. Since they feed mostly on the fruit of the *Pileus conica*, their plumage is sticky for much of the year.

St. Thomas Conure
(*A. pertinax pertinax*)

The forehead, cheeks, and chin are light orange-yellow, and there is a narrow yellow forehead band. The crown is green. The throat and upper part of the breast are olive green-yellow, which merges into orange-yellow on the belly. The back is green. The flight feathers are bluish, with black edges. The underside of the wings is yellowish-green and black. The upper side of the long tail is

The St. Thomas conure *(Aratinga pertinax pertinax)* is an affectionate bird that, unfortunately, has become rather scarce in aviculture.

green, with a blue tip (at least the central tail feathers), while the underside is gold-green. The eyes are brown, the eye ring is white, the feet are grayish-black to brown, Length: about 9¾ inches (25 cm); tail: 3½ to 4¾ inches (9–12 cm). The hen is frequently shorter: about 9 to 9¾ inches (23–25 cm). Weight: male, 3.4 ounces (96 g); hen, 3.2 ounces (91 g).

The subspecies originally came from Curacao and was probably imported into St. Thomas and St. Croix more than a century ago. Nests are frequently built in arboreal termite nests. The birds spend much of their time in trees (including plantations, where they are very destructive), especially on the mountain slopes. They live in small colonies. They are also known to dig out nests in sandy cliff faces. There are about 14 subspecies in the *pertinax* group.

This species has become quite scarce in aviculture, though in the past it was imported quite frequently. The birds are noisy, destructive, and aggressive toward other species. They can, however, become quite affectionate toward their keeper. The hen lays two to three eggs. The nest box should have dimensions of 13¾ x 13¾ x 6 inches (35 x 35 x 15 cm), with an entrance hole 2⅓ inch (6 cm) in diameter.

Guyana Brown-throated Conure or Orange-cheeked Conure
(A. p. chrysophrys)

The bird is primarily green, with a black-blueish crown and forehead. The wings are dark blue, black on the inner edges. There are small orange feathers around the eyes and sometimes also along the brown cheeks. There is a yellowish-brown or orange eye stripe. The throat is grayish-brown, the breast frequently a lighter brown to olive brown. The belly is yellowish-brown with a central orange stripe. The underside of the wings is yellowish-gray; lighter yellowish-gray under the tail. Length: about 9½ inches (24 cm). Weight: 2.5 ounces

The Guyana brown-throated conure *(Aratinga pertinax chrysophrys)* is rather noisy and destructive.

(71 g). The orange on the belly is usually absent in juveniles.

The subspecies *A. p. arubensis* (Aruba brown-throated conure) has a dark orange-yellow belly and a light yellow eye ring. The subspecies *A. p. xanthogenia* (Bonaire brown-throated conure) has more yellow in the crown above the eye and is lighter on the head. In my opinion, this is the best looking of the subspecies.

These birds are found in Guyana, Surinam, southeastern Venezuela and northern Brazil. They are regularly imported but have never become very popular, probably because of their unfavorable characteristics. They are noisy and destructive birds. Some individuals can be extremely aggressive toward other parrotlike birds, but others may be quite tolerant.

A single pair will usually breed enthusiastically in a roomy aviary. The nest box dimensions are 13¾ x 13¾ x 6 inches (35 x 35 x 15 cm), with an entrance hole 2⅓ inches (6 cm) in diameter. The box should be placed high in the aviary. The floor of the box should be covered with a layer of damp moss or mulm about 1½ inches (4 cm) thick.

The hen lays two to five eggs (28 by 21 millimeters), which take about 28 days to hatch. The young leave the nest 40–50 days after hatching. Personally, I have found much satisfaction with these birds, especially when it comes to breeding. Their good characteristics (color, readiness to breed, etc.) more than make up for the bad ones.

Brown-eared Conure or Veragua Conure *(A. p. ocularis)*

The throat and upper breast are brownish, the cheeks somewhat darker. The rest of the breast is light grass green. The abdomen is yellowish-green with orange. There is less blue on the front of the crown than in the brown-throated conure *(A. p. aeruginosa)*. The eye ring is light beige (especially conspicuous above the eye, where the naked skin is a little wider). The lower edge of the eye has an orange "eyelash" that can easily be seen. The underside of the wings is brown, frequently with some yellow. The underside of the tail is grayish with a yellow sheen; the upper side of the tail is dark green. The wings are bluish with black edges. The iris is light yellow. Length: 9½ inches (24 cm). Weight: 2.6 ounces (74 g). Juvenile birds do not have the beige eye ring and are green on the throat and breast.

The subspecies is native to Panama from the Gulf of Chiriqui to the Canal. It is regularly available on the market. The birds are fairly destructive and often remain nervous for a long time after capture. They require a large aviary with a steady supply of twigs to keep them busy (willow, beech, oak, fruit trees, etc.), a varied seed menu (avoid too many sunflower seeds) and green food. Millet and canary grass seed are also taken eagerly. Apples, other fruit, and rearing food can be given at all times of the year, but especially during the breeding season.

Brown-throated Conure *(A. p. aeruginosa)*

This subspecies is very similar in appearance to *A. p. arubensis*, but it has less yellow-brown on the

The brown-throated conure *(Aratinga pertinax aeruginosa)* has some orange-yellow in the abdomen.

head. It has a narrow orange-yellow ring around the eye. The abdomen is more orange-yellow. The brown color on the throat, breast, and sides of the head is somewhat darker. Length: about 9¾ inches (25 cm). Weight: 2.8 ounces (79 g).

The natural habitat of this subspecies extends from eastern Colombia to western Venezuela and northwestern Brazil (Rio Branco). This beautifully colored bird is available occasionally and gives few breeding difficulties. In 1908 the first (three) young were raised in England. The juveniles were raised on a diet of milk-soaked stale-bread, soaked canary grass seed, and a rich variety of green food and fruit.

Top: The austral or Magellan conure *(Enicognathus ferrugineus)* is rather common throughout its range. The birds were first bred in the East Berlin Zoo in the early 1970s.
Bottom: The greater Patagonian conure *(Cyanoliseus patagonus byroni)*, left, and the lesser Patagonian conure *(C. p. patagonus)*, right, live in colonies, and often excavate their nest tunnels in the limestone rocks of the Andes and Cordilleras.

South American Conure Species

Margarita Brown-throated Conure
(A. p. margaritensis)

This subspecies is similar in color to the preceding one, but with less or no orange on the abdomen. The head is like that of the gold-fronted conure, with the exception of the cheek, the area between the eye, and throat, which is brown. The forehead is whitish. A little orange shimmers in the cheeks. The throat and upper part of the breast are pale olive. Length: 10 inches (25.5 cm). Weight: 9.7 ounces (275 g).

The birds are native to the Island of Margarita, and the Paria peninsula on the mainland. They are quite common in the hills and lowlands along the coast, living in groups of 8 to 20. In the wild the birds breed mainly in termite mounds: the hen lays three to five eggs.

Cactus Conure
(A. cactorum cactorum)

This species is similar in appearance to the Guyana brown-throated conure but has some blue on the brownish crown, and the brown feathers have light edges. The area between beak and eye, the cheeks, the sides of the neck, and the upper part of the breast are light greenish-brown. There is frequently a yellow stripe above the eye. The feathers around the ears are light green. The lower belly is usually dark orange-yellow, the older the bird, the richer the color. The flanks, the thighs, and the undertail coverts are greenish-yellow; the wing feathers are blue with black tips. The back is green. The central tail feathers are blue; the underside of the tail is gold-green. Upper mandible is white, lower mandible light horn-colored. Length: about

Top: Like all other Pyrrhura species, the painted conure (*Pyrrhura p. picta*) needs a roomy aviary and a nest box for the night.
Bottom: The maroon-bellied conure (*P. f. frontalis*) has forests, farmland, orchards, and corn fields as its habitat. Once accustomed to captivity, they will grow very affectionate.

The cactus conure *(Aratinga c. cactorum)* is well-known in aviculture. The Brazilian aviculturist Nelse Kawall has a yellow mutation of this species in his collection.

9¾ inches (25 cm). Weight: 3.2 ounces (91 g). Juveniles have a green crown and an olive green throat and breast. The orange color may already be apparent on the belly.

The subspecies *A. c. caixana*, which occurs in eastern Brazil, is difficult to distinguish from the nominate form. It is somewhat paler, and the brown color on the throat and breast is a little deeper. Both subspecies often get "mixed up" in the trade.

According to Rosemary Low, the nominate species comes from Brazil (Bahia, southwards to Rio São Francisco and surrounding areas in Minas Geraës). This bird derives its name from the fact that the main part of its diet consists of cactus fruits. In the wild the birds live in groups.

These birds can become tame and affectionate pets. They are not particularly destructive and are relatively quiet compared with other members of the genus. They require a large aviary for successful breeding. I bred a pair successfully in a nest box with the dimensions 9¾ x 19½ x 11¾ inches (25 x 50 x 30 cm), with an entrance hole 2⅓ inches (6 cm) in diameter.

The hen lays three to four eggs, which hatch after 25 days. The young leave the nest after about 48 days but are somewhat dependent on their parents for a few days more.

As extra food the birds can be given pieces of fresh, sweet apple, millet spray, pieces of melon, figs, berries, soaked seeds (especially in the breeding season), a rich variety of green food, and a good seed mixture.

Peach-fronted, Golden-crowned or Half-Moon Conure *(A. aurea aurea)*

This bird is similar in appearance to Petz's conure. It has a light gray-greenish back, with lighter green beneath, sometimes olive green, especially on the upper breast. The forehead and part of the crown and the feathers around the eyes and upper mandible are bright orange. The rest of the crown is blue-green. The cheeks and throat are

The Nanday conure *(Aratinga* or *Nandayus nenday)* is sexually mature in its third year.

The peach-fronted conure *(Aratinga a. aurea)* occurs in pairs or small groups in the wild.

olive green-yellow. The wings are gray-bluish with black tips. The tail is gray-greenish with a blue tip; the underside is yellowish-green. The beak is black. In my experience, the young first get the orange color of the eye ring at almost two years of age. Length: about 9¾ inches (25 cm). Weight: 3.7 ounces (105 g). A larger form, *A. a. major*, occurs at two localities approximately 75 miles (120 km) apart, on the banks of the Paraguay river in northern Paraguay to southern Bolivia, southwestern Mato Grosso, and northwestern Argentina.

The peach-fronted conure has the greatest natural range of all conures with the exception of the white-eyed conure. It is native to Brazil south of the Amazon and eastward to Rio Madeira, eastern Bolivia, Mato Grosso, and São Paulo. The birds live in pairs or small groups (10 to 20 birds), spending most of the day in trees and shrubs or on the ground foraging for seeds and fruit.

These well-known birds are fairly destructive and very noisy but, in spite of this, quite popular.

South American Conure Species

They breed fairly readily if given an aviary of sufficient length. The hen lays two to four eggs, which are incubated for 26 days. I have had many successes using a nest box 13¾ inches (35 cm) long, about 9¾ inches (25 cm) wide, and 9¾ inches (25 cm) high, with an entrance hole about 3¼ inches (8 cm) in diameter. The young leave the nest after about 52 days. Hybrids with cactus, Jenday, and monk conures have occurred.

These birds are aggressive during the breeding season and are best kept in single pairs. If housed next to other parrotlike species, they should be separated by double mesh to prevent possible injuries. A fancier in Brazil possesses a blue and two cinnamon mutations of this species.

Nanday Conure
(A. nenday or Nandayus nenday)

The top of the head, cheeks, and throat are blue-black, forming a cap of sorts. At the level of the eye, an area of greenish-yellow runs into the cap. The rest of the body is green (deeper on the breast, lighter on the wings). The flight feathers are bluish-black. The belly is rose-red. The tail is olive-green with bluish-black tip. The underside of the tail is green. The iris is dark reddish-brown, the beak blackish-gray, and the feet are brownish-gray. The eye ring is flesh colored. Length: about 11¾ to 12¼ inches (30–31 cm). Weight: 5.2 ounces (147 g).

This species is native to southeastern Bolivia, southern Mato Grosso, northern Argentina, Chaco Formosa, and Paraguay. The birds live in large flocks, often together with monk parakeets.

These birds will breed readily in captivity in a suitable aviary. They become sexually mature at three years of age. The hen lays two to six eggs, which are incubated for 24 to 26 days. The cock usually sits on or at the nest box. During the breeding period the birds must have a good food with calcium and mineral supplements (see Feeding, page 20).

These attractive birds quickly acclimate to their surroundings, and can be kept outside all year

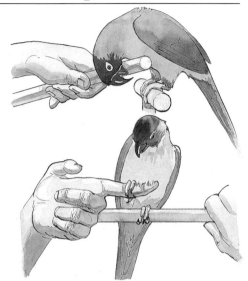

All conures make excellent pets. To train your conure to perch on your finger, make the bird sit on a "hand-hold" perch by pressing it softly against the abdomen. The next step is to move the index finger against the abdomen just above the legs. Press softly and carefully. The bird (in the illustration a Nanday conure) will usually oblige by seating itself on the outstretched finger.

round. A nest box 15¾ x 15¾ x 9¾ inches (40 x 40 x 25 cm), with an entrance hole 2¾ inches (7 cm) in diameter, should be offered. Nest inspections are best kept to a minimum. I have had the best breeding successes with a single pair in an aviary 2.5 x 13 x 6.7 feet (.75 x 4 x 2 m).

Nanday conures are fairly sociable birds, even with other species, but they have one drawback: they have a very loud, piercing screech that makes them unsuitable as house pets and can annoy your neighbors (and you!) even in a town garden aviary. Once tame and used to their surroundings, they do get a little quieter, but, in general, they are best suited to fanciers who live in the country or who have very large gardens. For those who can tolerate the noise, they make reasonable and affectionate pets which will feed from the fingers and can learn to repeat a few words.

South American Conure Species

Genus: *Brotogeris*

These green-colored parakeets have narrow tails and long, pointed wings that cover the tail. Some species are imported regularly every year and make ideal aviary birds. Some of them also make excellent pets. In the wild the birds usually nest in termite mounds.

Hand-reared specimens make friendly and affectionate pets, though some species have raucous and loud voices (canary-winged and white-winged parakeets, for example). Most of the species like a good bath, and you can give them much pleasure in the summer by regularly spraying them lightly with a garden hose. All birds in this genus sleep in a nest box even outside the breeding season. Since most species rarely come to the ground, you should place their food and water containers at least 5 feet (1.5 m) from the ground on a platform or shelf.

Plain, All-Green or Tirica Parakeet
(*B. tirica*)

This species is wholly green, with a little yellow on the upper side and blue wing feathers. The central tail feathers also have a bluish tinge. Length: 9 inches (23 cm); tail: 4 to 6 inches (10–15 cm). Weight: 2.0 ounces (57 g).

The Tirica parakeet is found in eastern and southeastern Brazil (southern Bahia to São Paolo and inland to southern Goias). The species is quite abundant in its native lands as well as in our aviaries. The first examples were imported into Germany in 1873, and the first breeding successes were reported in 1882. Today regular shipments of these birds still arrive in Europe and North America. A blue mutation has been reported from Brazil. The hen lays four to five eggs (19 x 15 millimeters); the incubation time is 22 to 23 days.

White-winged Parakeet
(*B. versicolurus versicolurus*)

This species is very similar in appearance to the canary-winged parakeet, but the white-winged para-

The white-winged parakeet *(Brotogeris v. versicolurus)* is grayer and more olive-colored, especially on the head, than the canary-winged parakeet.

keet is grayer and more olive, especially on the head. There is a blue sheen around the eyes. There is a white bar (from which the name arises) with a yellow tinge in the wings, but the latter is less obvious than in the canary-winged parakeet. Usually, the white is visible only when the wings are spread. Length: 8⅔ inches (22 cm). Weight: 2.1 ounces (60 g).

White-winged parakeets are native to French Guiana, through the Amazon valley, to eastern Ecuador and northeastern Peru. They are also found on the islands of Pará and Mexicana, have been introduced on Puerto Rico, and probably occur in Surinam. In some areas they may be encountered in their hundreds along the rivers at dusk.

This species is imported regularly. It is not particularly noisy. Tame birds are adept talkers. Pairs can sometimes break out into a duet of screaming and settle down again in a few minutes. The species can be kept safely in a community aviary with other small birds (but not psittacines). The birds are not particularly destructive. They sometimes hang like bats from the roof of the aviary. Nest box: 9¾ x 9¾ x 13¾ inches (25 x 25 x 35 cm) with an entrance hole 2¾ inches (7 cm) in diameter. They are usually somewhat aggressive during the breeding season. A blue mutation is reported from Brazil.

Canary-winged Parakeet
(*B. v. chiriri*)

The body is mainly green, darker above than underneath, where there is a black and yellow shimmer. There is a bright yellow epaulet on the wings. The beak is light horn colored, and the iris is dark brown. Length: 8½ to 8⅔ inches (21.5–22 cm). Weight: 2.1 ounces (60 g).

The canary-winged parakeet is native to northern and eastern Bolivia, northern Argentina (Chaco, Missiones), Paraguay, and São Paolo. This probably is the most widely imported bird of all South American psittacines; it was exhibited in the London zoo as early as 1868. Over the years it has turned out to be an exemplary aviary inmate. The hen lays three to five eggs, occasionally six (22 to 23 by 18 to 19 millimeters), and incubates them unaided for about 26 days. The young leave the nest at about two months of age. A good variety of green food is necessary throughout the year, but especially at breeding time. Grass and weed seeds, apples, pears, cherries, soaked raisins, and bananas can supplement the diet.

It is unfortunate that these beautiful parakeets have such a nerve-shattering voice (used when they are not wholly contented), but they should not be too much trouble if kept in a roomy outdoor aviary. The best kind of nest box is a tough natural birchwood log. Alternatively, you can use a homemade box with the dimension 17¾ x 9¾ x 9¾ inches (45 x 25 x 25 cm). A layer of humus or peat about 1.6 inches (4 cm) thick should be laid at the bottom. The box should be affixed high in the aviary for best results. The birds can winter in the outdoor aviary provided they have a draft-free, dry shelter.

Orange-chinned, Tovi or Bee-Bee Parakeet (*B. jugularis jugularis*)

The primary color is green, with a yellow sheen on the underside and blue on the lower belly. There is a little blue on the head, back, rump, wings, and tail. There is a round orange mark on the chin. The underside of the wings is yellowish, the flight feathers are blue, the beak is light horn colored. Length: to about 7⅛ inches (18 cm). Weight: 2.2 ounces (62 g).

The birds range from southwestern Mexico to Northern Colombia, west of the eastern Andes, and eastward to Notre Santander. They usually live in partially open habitats in groups of about 20 individuals, but sometimes in single pairs. They feed freely on nectar but also on flowers, fruit and half-ripe seeds. They have particular resting and roosting sites, where hundreds of birds may gather. They breed in termite mounds and in tree hollows, often in dead limbs. Sometimes two or more pairs may breed in the same tree. A clutch of eight to nine eggs is not unusual. The incubation time is about 22 days.

Although these parakeets are relatively easy to breed in captivity, they are not bred as much as they should be (probably because inexpensive imported birds are usually available). The genuine fancier on a limited budget thus has the opportunity to study the breeding habits of this charming bird. Clutches in captivity usually are smaller than in the wild (three to four eggs per clutch), but a pair may frequently rear two or three clutches per year. During breeding, a diet of soaked corn, rice, fruit, fresh twigs and buds, and soaked stale bread (with the excess water squeezed out) should be given in addition to their normal seed and green-food diet. The birds should always have access to a sleeping/nesting box: 11¾ x 11¾ x 15¾ inches (30 x 30 x 40 cm), with a 3¼-inch (8-cm) entrance hole. Newly imported birds remain nervous for a while, but they soon settle down and, with kindness and patience, can be finger tamed quite easily.

Gray-cheeked, Orange-flanked or Orange-winged Parakeet
(B. pyrrhopterus)

This species is primarily green, lighter on the belly. The crown is grayish, the forehead and cheeks are pale gray. There are orange patches both above and below the wings. Length: 7⅞ inches (20 cm). Weight: 2.1 ounces (60 g).

Gray-cheeked parakeets are native to western South America, from Bahia de Caráques to north-western Peru. They frequently form large flocks and can cause severe damage to banana and other plantations.

These parakeets are frequently available in the trade and are often kept as pet birds. They should have conditions similar to those described for the Tovi parakeet. Hybridization with the Tovi Parakeet is possible. According to the ornithologist Barrett, these birds nest in termite mounds, but will also use a hollow limb. Four to six eggs (20 to 22 by 16 to 18 millimeters) are laid on a layer of damp moss. The hen incubates the eggs unaided, but the cock keeps guard close to the nest.

These birds have an interesting habit of assembling in huge flocks at certain times of the year, just like starlings. They are quite intelligent little birds; with patience you can teach them to repeat a few words, or even to "cry" or "laugh."

A breeding pair should have access to a nest box 13¾ x 11¾ x 11¾ inches (35 x 30 x 30 cm) in size with an entrance 3⅛ inches in diameter. A thick layer (2⅓ to 3 ¼ inches, or 6–8 cm) of damp moss, peat, or similar material should be placed on the floor of the box. The box should be affixed as high as possible, with the entrance facing the north. The birds should be kept in individual pairs for breeding, but other small birds (such as finches, doves, and quail) may be kept with them without any problem.

Cobalt-winged, Blue-winged, or De Ville's Parakeet (B. c. cyanoptera)

This is another predominantly green species with a little blue sheen on the head and neck. Frequently there is a yellow eye stripe, and the chin is orange. The secondary flight feathers are blue, the underside of the wings is blue-green, and the central tail feathers are blue. The beak is horn colored; there is a naked white eye ring; and the iris is dark brown. The feet are flesh colored. Length: 7⅞ inches (20 cm). Weight: 2.2 ounces (62 g).

This species is native to Venezuela, Colombia, and the upper part of the Amazon Basin. The birds are found at altitudes of up to 6,600 feet (2,000 m) in the hills of the tropical rain forests, where they live in small groups high in the trees.

These birds are sensitive to frost and must not be kept below 53° F (12° C). They should always have access to a sleeping/breeding box, in which they will spend their nights. The hen usually lays four to five eggs—occasionally six—which are incubated for 23 to 24 days. The young leave the nest after seven to eight weeks but are still fed by their parents for about a month.

Golden-winged Parakeet
(B. c. chrysopterus)

This is a primarily green parakeet with a brownish patch on the chin. The primary flight feathers are deep orange. The undersides of the wings are blue. The beak is light horn colored. Length: about 6⅓ inches (16 cm). Weight: 1.7 ounces (48 g).

Golden-winged parakeets occur in eastern Venezuela, Guyana, Surinam, and French Guiana to the northern Amazon area. They are especially common along the coast of Guyana in coffee plantations, where they feed on the flowers of *Erythrina* trees.

They nest in hollow limbs, laying two to four eggs. In captivity they seem to be "difficult" breeders, thus posing a challenge for the more enthusiastic fancier.

South American Conure Species

Tuipara Parakeet *(B. c. tuipara)*

This subspecies is mainly green in color, with a lighter underside. There is a blue-black sheen on the head. There is a yellow-orange stripe across the forehead and an orange stripe on the chin. There are yellow feathers on the wings and on the tail. The primary flight feathers are a shiny blue-black, edged with dark green. The eyes are brown, with a naked, greenish-blue eye ring. The beak is whitish-gray, and the feet are pink. Length: about 7⅛ inches (18 cm); tail: 2⅓ to 3¼ inches (6–8 cm). Weight: 2.0 ounces (57 g).

Tuipara parakeets are found in the lower Amazon basin and along the northern Brazilian coast, sometimes in groups of about 40 individuals. They feed largely on the fruit of the tree *Bombax monguba*.

This species is available only occasionally from the better importers. It is unquestionably an extremely enticing bird worth our attention. It soon becomes tame, but has a rather overbearing screech. It is best suited to a roomy outdoor aviary with minimum dimensions of 13 x 8 x 6½ feet (4 x 2.5 x 2 m) and should have access to a nest box with dimensions of 8⅔ x 8⅔ x 19½ inches (22 x 22 x 50 cm). It can be kept in a community aviary with other species (finches, doves, quail, etc.). Since the birds climb and clamber a lot, they should be given natural branches and twigs to keep them amused.

Tui Parakeet
(B. sactithomae sactithomae)

This bird is primarily bright green, with a lighter (yellow) underside. The forehead, the front portion of the crown, and the area below the eyes are yellow. The slender wings have a shading of blue. The underside of the tail is green with a yellow tinge. The beak is shiny chestnut-colored; the feet are flesh colored. Length: 6.7 inches (17 cm). Weight: 1.7 ounces (49.5 g).

The Tui parakeet occurs in eastern Ecuador, northeastern Peru, and eastward to western Brazil, northern Bolivia, and parts of Amazonian Colombia. In the wild it nests in termite mounds as well as hollow trees. The hen lays four to six eggs, which she incubates for 21 days. The young leave the nest after 45 days.

This species, which is available on a regular basis, is known for its peaceful and trusting nature. Surprisingly, however, these are not the easiest birds to breed in captivity. They require a nest box 8⅔ x 8⅔ x 24 inches (22 x 22 x 60 cm), in size, with an entrance hole 2¾ inches (7 cm) in diameter.

Genus *Enicognathus*

Austral or Magellan Conure
(E. f. ferrugineus)

This species is mainly green, with most of the feathers darkly edged. The forehead and eye stripe are red. There is a bluish sheen on the crown. There is a reddish-brown patch on the belly. The beak is black, the naked eye ring is blackish-gray, the iris is reddish-brown, and the feet are gray. Length: 14⅗ inches (37 cm). Weight: 4.9 ounces (139 g).

Magellan conures are native to southern Argentina (Tierra del Fuego) and Chile around the southernmost tip of South America. They live mainly in woodlands but also in parks and other cultivated areas. They sometimes appear in fairly large flocks. The hen usually lays four to seven eggs (about 31 by 25 millimeters). Although the birds were imported into Europe in 1866, they are relatively scarce in aviculture.

The better-known subspecies, the Chilean conure *(E. f. minor)*, grows to 13⅓ inches (34 cm) and is available more frequently than the nominate form. It is somewhat darker than the Magellan conure. This includes the red forehead band and the red belly patch, which can be so dark as to virtually disappear in the darker green. The bird is found in southwestern Argentina and southern Chile. In Europe it can breed as late as December. The hen lays two to six eggs, which are incubated for 21 to 27 days. The young leave the nest after six to eight weeks.

This species is recognized as an excellent aviary bird with a not-too-unpleasant voice, which it likes to exercise toward evening. It has quite a good name as a household pet. The birds like to forage on the ground, so occasional seeds sprinkled on the aviary floor will please them. A good night shelter is advisable and a sleeping box with the dimensions 24 x 19½ x 17¾ inches (60 x 50 x 45 cm).

Long-billed or Slender-billed Conure (*E. leptorhynchus*)

This species is green, with an olive-colored belly. The flight feathers are bluish. The feathers are edged with a dull brown border. The forehead, cheeks, eye stripe, lower belly, and tail are brownish-red. The long, narrow, flat, black, upper mandible (twice as long as the lower mandible) is striking. This beak is used for raking into the ground in search of seeds, roots, and other food items. (One of the main seeds eaten in the wild is that of the *Araucaria* pine.) The iris is yellow-brown, and the feet brownish-black. Length: 15¾ inches (40 cm). Weight: 5.4 ounces (153 g).

Long-billed conures are found in central Chile, mainly in wooded country, in noisy groups of 50–300 birds. In spring they move into the mountains to an altitude of 6,600 feet (2,000 m) or more. Sometimes they fly in line formations some 200 feet (60 m) long, depending on the number of birds.

In the wild the hen lays about four eggs, which she incubates alone. The cock stands guard close by. In captivity they are relatively peaceful birds, which soon become tame and affectionate. During the summer they appreciate a water bath.

The birds should be kept in a roomy outdoor aviary with a draft-free, dry night shelter. The flight should be at least 13 x 16 feet (4–5 m) long for these active birds. Since they frequently forage on the ground, they should be checked for worms (fecal examination by a veterinarian) at regular

The long-billed conure (*Enicognathus leptorhynchus*) has a narrow and straight upper mandible, protruding beyond the lower mandible.

intervals and treated if necessary. They should have permanent access to a sleeping box 24 x 19½ x 17¾ inches (60 x 50 x 45 cm) or a natural nest log (best placed in the night shelter). The entrance hole should be 3½ inches (9 cm) in diameter.

These birds are not aggressive toward members of their own species or others in the genus. Thus they can be kept with the other *Enicognathus* species in a large aviary, though pairs are best kept alone for breeding. Some thick perches, about 2 to 2⅓ inches (5–6 cm) in diameter, will be appreciated by the birds. They should be fed on a diet of millet, canary grass seeds, oats, hemp, corn, and sunflower seeds, plus fruit (apples) and greens (including carrots and root vegetables). Some individuals will eagerly take mealworms and may be given a few each day. The seeds can also be offered germinated or sown on the floor of the aviary.

Good breeding results have been obtained in cages with a minimum size of 36 x 24 x 24 inches (90 x 60 x 90 cm). Usually, two to four eggs are laid, and they are incubated for 26 to 27 days. The young fledge at seven to eight weeks. The dimensions of the nest box should be 30 x 19½ x 17¾ inches (75 x 50 x 45 cm).

South American Conure Species

Genus *Cyanoliseus*

These beautiful birds are ideal aviary inmates but, because of their loud, nerve-shattering voices, are perhaps better left to bird fanciers with a large garden aviary. In Argentina the greater Patagonian conure is known as the "bank-burrowing parrot," since it burrows a depth of 6 feet (1.8 m) into the side of a cliff or a bank to nest. These birds are all very sociable, living in large colonies and nesting close together.

Patagonian or Lesser Patagonian Conure *(C. patagonus patagonus)*

The upper side is olive-brown. The rump, undersides, and flanks are whitish yellow, with an olive green sheen. The throat and breast are ash-brown, frequently sprinkled with white feathers, which sometimes form a band around the bend of the wing. In the center of the belly there is deep orange-red color; the rest of the belly is yellow. The shoulder feathers are olive green; the wing feathers blue with black tips. The tail is olive green above, brown beneath. The beak is gray-black; the eye ring is white. Length: 17¾ inches (45 cm). Weight: 8.3 ounces (235 g).

The Patagonian conure *(Cyanoliseus p. patagonus)* is often called burrowing parakeet, for obvious reasons.

The Patagonian conure ranges from southern to central Argentina, occasionally into Uruguay. It feeds mainly on fruit, berries (especially those of *Empetrum rubrum*), and all kinds of seeds (including those of the giant thistle *Carduus mariana*). The birds live together in groups throughout the year and nest close together in holes in inaccessible rock faces.

During the last few years these birds have become very popular in aviculture, although their voices are loud and piercing. Sometimes they are kept as pets, since they are fairly good mimics. Breeding behavior is similar to that of the greater Patagonian conure (below). The hen lays three to four eggs, which hatch after 24 to 26 days.

Greater Patagonian Conure *(C. p. byroni)*

This bird is somewhat larger than the Patagonian conure and has a more robust beak. Some specimens have an almost complete white band around the bend of the wing and across the breast. Length: 19 inches (48 cm). Weight: 8.7 ounces (247 g). The greater Patagonian conure comes from a small area of Chile in the foothills of the Andes and along the coast (between Atacama and Colchagua). Like the nominate subspecies, these birds live in colonies and lay their eggs on the bare rocks in cliff hollows. According to A. W. Johnson (*The Birds of Chile*, Vol. II), in springtime (October to November) the natives climb the cliffs and remove the young from their nests with long bamboo poles with a hook at the end. The young birds are then hand reared and tamed, ready to sell to the international livestock traders.

In spite of their loud, screeching calls, these birds are much sought after as pets. Unfortunately, the collection of birds, as mentioned above, is a serious threat to their status in the wild. In captivity the subspecies has been successfully bred on a number of occasions, usually in a large aviary. The best type of nesting facility in captivity is a hollow log with an inner diameter of 11¾ inches (30 cm) and about 2 feet (95 cm) deep. The birds will gnaw at the interior walls, forming a bed of wood chips on which the eggs will be laid.

The hen lays three to four eggs, which are incubated for about 25 days. The young leave the nest at about eight weeks of age and are already quite agile, trailing their parents in and out of the nest. At first the upper mandible of the young is whitish, becoming black at about eight months of age. The cock assists in the feeding of the young. These beautiful birds can be kept well on a diet including safflower and sunflower seeds, canary grass seeds, millet, some hemp, raisins, apples, bread (softened in water and squeezed out), green food, chickweed, and fruit. Most of these birds are very fond of spinach.

Genus *Pyrrhura*

Many members of this interesting genus are not often seen on the market, which is a shame because they are very beautiful birds and not nearly as noisy as *Aratinga* species. They are also minimally destructive, especially if regularly supplied with fresh twigs to occupy their attention.

Blue-throated Conure *(P. cruentata)*

There are chestnut brown ear patches with orange-brown spots just behind them. The feathers of the forehead, crown, and first part of the neck are edged in orange. The cheeks are green, and there is a chestnut brown stripe from the beak to the eye. There is a blue half-ring in the nape, and the upper part of the breast also has a bluish tinge. There is a red patch on the belly, and auburn markings on the abdomen. The wing patch is carmine red, and the primary flight feathers are edged with blue and green. The tail is yellowish green with red. The underside of the tail is dull brownish red. The beak is black. Length: 9½ inches (24 cm). Weight: 2.9 ounces (82 g).

The species is found along the coast of Brazil to northeastern São Paolo. It is protected in the wild

The painted conure *(Pyrrhura p. picta)* is one of the most active and interesting species of its genus!

and is available only occasionally. The specimens I have dealt with have always been quiet and affectionate. Breeding successes have been reported in not-too-large, well-protected aviaries. The birds are best kept in single pairs.

J. Spenkelink van Schaik reported that the best breeding pairs laid seven to eight eggs per clutch. This species has also been successfully bred in Walsrode, Germany. It is the largest of the genus and perhaps also the most colorful, making it extremely useful to breed. For further details regarding husbandry, see the following species.

Painted Conure *(P. picta picta)*

This species is mainly green and does not have the forehead band. It is very similar to *P. leucotis* (see following), but is about 1 inch (2 cm) shorter. The forehead and crown are light blue. The back of the head is black. It has cream-colored ear patches. The pattern on the neck and head is like a "closed, accoladelike edge," with a fine network of markings. This is in contrast to other members of the genus, in which each feather is more or less edged. The name "picta" (painted) is thus well chosen. The wing joint is light red. The tail is reddish brown, close to copper red. The belly and rump are reddish brown. The outer primaries are blue. The iris is brown. Length: 8⅔ inches (22 cm). Weight: 2.6 ounces (74 g).

The species is native to Surinam, Guyana and the Amazon basin. Few breeding successes have been reported in captivity, but, according to J. Spenkeling (personal communication), they are generally good breeding birds. They require a thick-walled nest box or, if possible, a natural, hollow log with minimum dimensions of 11¾ x 11¾ x 15¾ inches (30 x 30 x 40 cm) and an entrance diameter 2¾ inches (7 cm). In Europe the birds want to nest very early, sometimes even in December. A pair is thus best kept in a roomy aviary, with a minimum flight length of 12 feet (4 m), with a draft-free, dry night shelter.

I kept a pair for some time in the Netherlands. They were extremely active and reared one clutch per year, in a birch log of the dimensions described above. The hen laid four to five eggs, but usually only two to three of these were fertile. The incubation time was 26 to 27 days. The young left the nest 31 to 32 days later but were still fed by the parents for two to two-and-a-half weeks.

White-eared Conure
(P. leucotis leucotis)

This species is mainly dark green, with a dark brown forehead and cheeks. The crown and the collar are deep dark brown; there is a little blue in the neck. The ear patches are pale beige. The breast feathers are black with white edges. There is a striking chestnut brown patch on the belly and on the back, to the first tail coverts. The wing patch is orange-red, and there is some dull red beneath the wing. The primary flight feathers have blue edges. The long tail is chestnut brown with a greenish tint at the bases and yellowish red underneath. The

The white-eared conure *(Pyrrhura l. leucotis)* lives in the region of Rio de Janeiro and São Paolo.

beak is brownish-gray. Length: 8⅓ inches (21 cm). Weight: 2.3 ounces (65 g).

In recent times Emma's Conure *(P. l. emma)* from Venezuela (from Caracas eastwards to Sucre) has been available. It is larger, has more blue on the head and has a reddish-brown forehead, this color running over the crown. It also has some blue in the cheeks, the neck and the throat. There have been some breeding reports. Incubation time is about 23 days and the young fledge at 30–32 days, but continue to be fed by the parents for two or three weeks.

The white-eared conure is native to Brazilian coastal areas, where it lives in woodlands and at wood edges, especially in the regions of Rio de Janeiro and São Paolo. It has been imported into Europe since 1871. The birds breed regularly in the aviary. The hen lays three to eight eggs. The incubation period is about 20 days, and the young leave the nest at about seven weeks. The nest box dimensions are 9¾ x 13¾ inches (25 x 35 cm), with an entrance hole 2⅓ inches in diameter. For further details, see the maroon-bellied conure (page 76).

South American Conure Species

Crimson-bellied Conure
(*P. perlata rhodogaster*)

The crown and forehead are dark, brownish-gray, the latter with a small blue band. The areas of the ears are lighter. The throat and neck are light gray, with lighter-edged feathers. The upper breast feathers are edged with blue-gray (scallop markings). The area of the beak to the eyes is greenish-blue. The collar, tail coverts, and underside are blue. The wings and back are dark green. The breast and belly are scarlet (still green in juveniles). There is a red patch on the wings, which are also reddish beneath. The primary flight feathers are blue. The tail is chestnut brown above, black beneath. The beak, the iris, and the feet are grayish black. Length: 9½ inches (24 cm). Weight: 2.8 ounces (79 g).

The crimson-bellied conure is native to a small area of northern Brazil bounded by two tributaries of the Amazon (Madeira and Tapayas Rivers in the east and the Jamouchin River in the west) as well as to the Mato Grosso.

The crimson-bellied conure *(Pyrrhura perlata rhodogaster)* is a very tolerant bird in a roomy garden aviary.

These are very sociable, affectionate, and curious birds. They like to sleep in a large nest box 9¾ x 9¾ x 11¾ inches (25 x 25 x 30 cm). Since they are adept at escaping, the aviary mesh should be checked regularly. They breed regularly in captivity. The hen lays three to five eggs (see the maroon-bellied conure, below, for further information). They should be given adequate twigs and branches to gnaw at. During the fall and winter months, the birds are best kept indoors in a roomy flight at least 10 feet (3 m) long. This species is very tolerant in a large community aviary.

Maroon-bellied Conure
(*P. frontalis frontalis*)

There is a chestnut-red band on the forehead and a more or less broad stripe just above the nose. The rest of the top of the head is dark green, while the feathers on the neck are lighter edged. The ear patch is a light dull brown. Length: 10¼ inches (26 cm). Weight: 3.2 ounces (91 g).

This species comes from southeastern Brazil, from the east of Minas Geraes and Espirito Santo to Rio de Janeiro. It is also found in northeastern Argentina, Uruguay, and eastern Paraguay. The species is available irregularly at any time of the year.

The maroon-bellied conure is an ideal species for the beginner. The birds breed readily, sometimes raising several broods per season, and are not difficult to care for. Give them a normal parakeet seed mixture plus fruit and green food.

These birds do not demand much room and will live in a lovebird cage, though this is far from ideal. The maroon-bellied conure is one of the hardiest of the South American birds and readily adapts to our climate. It is also more resistant to worm infections than Australian parakeets.

This species can be kept in a group, but the birds should be separated into individual pairs for breeding. I like to place a number of unrelated individuals together and let them choose their own partners.

Maroon-bellied conures are ready to breed at one year of age. They prefer a natural, hollow log about 19½ inches (50 cm) deep as a nest box. The inside can have dimensions similar to those recommended for *Neophema* species (see above). Such a log is prefered to a box by all *Pyrrhura* species. Outside the breeding season, they should retain their box for sleeping, otherwise they will get frostbite on their toes. A hiding place also helps them lose their shyness more quickly. I put some partly rotted wood pulp on the floor of the box. The hen gnaws this up into a fine bed for the eggs.

The clutch sometimes is quite large: seven to nine eggs is quite normal for this species. If they get an early start (February, for example), the birds will most probably rear a second brood. The incubation period is about 28 days (a few days longer in very cold weather), and the young are ready to leave the nest in another 60 days. Two days after fledging, the young are more or less independent, but I like to leave mine with their parents for a while.

Inbreeding is deleterious to the health and viability of future offspring. Try therefore, not to mate offspring from one pair, but endeavor to obtain fresh blood by exchange with other fanciers. It would be a great shame to lose all captive stock by continued inbreeding. In my opinion, there are enough specimens in Europe, the United States, and Canada for good unrelated stock to be bred and maintained without the necessity of further imports.

Maroon-tailed or Black-tailed Conure (*P. melanura melanura*)

The forehead is brown; the brown feathers on the crown are edged with green. Ear coverts are green. The upper part of the breast, the throat, and sides of the neck are brownish-green, the feathers being lighter edged. The rest of the breast is dark green, with some chestnut red feathers on the lower belly. There is red in the primary flight feathers, with yellow tips and yellow feathers (which are covered by the red feathers so as to be almost invisible). The tail is black, with a green base and dark chestnut brown on the underside. The beak is horn-colored, and there is a large, white eye ring. The iris is dark brown, and the feet are light gray. Length: 9½ inches (24 cm). Weight: 2.8 ounces (79 g).

This species occurs in the northwestern Amazon region, to the upper Orinoco (Rio Cunucunuma), eastward to Rio Negro, and southward to northeastern Peru (Pebas) and the Rio Solimoës.

Since 1970 this species has been regularly available in the trade, especially in the United States and Germany. It requires care similar to that of the maroon-bellied conure (see above) but is probably not as interesting. It breeds readily in captivity. The nest box should be 13¾ inches (35 cm) deep and 9¾ inches (25 cm) square. Place a layer of damp mulm at the base. The incubation time is about 26 days. The young leave the nest after about seven weeks.

The marooned-tailed conure *(Pyrrhura m. melanura)* is a regularly available bird and makes an excellent pet.

Useful Addresses and Literature

Avicultural Societies

Canada
British Columbia Avicultural Society
11784-90th Avenue
North Delta, British Columbia V4C 3H6
The Canadian Avicultural Society
32 Dronmore Court
Williwdale, Ontario M2R 2H5
Canadian Parrot Association
Pine Oaks R.R. #3
St. Catharines, Ontario L2R 6P9

Great Britain
The Avicultural Society
The Secretary
Warren Hill, Halford's Lane
Hartley Wintney
Hampshire RG27 8AG
The European Aviculture Council
c/o Mr. Dave Axtell
P.O. Box 74
Bury St. Edmunds, Suffolk IP30 OHS

United States
American Federation of Aviculture
P.O. Box 56218
Phoenix, AZ 85079-6218
Avicultural Society of America
P.O. Box 2196
Redondo Beach, CA 90218
National Parrot Association
8 North Hoffmann Lane
Hauppauge, NY 11788
Association of Avian Veterinarians
5770 Lake Worth Road
Lake Worth, FL 33463-3299

Books

Forshaw, Joseph M. *Parrots of the World*, 3rd
edition, Lansdowne, Melbourne, Australia,
1989.
Low, Rosemary *The Complete Book of Parrots,*
Barron's Educational Series, Hauppauge, New
York, 1989.
————*Parrots: Their Care and Breeding*, 2nd edi-
tion, Blandford Press, London, New York,
Sydney, 1986.
————*The Parrots of South America*, John Gifford,
London, 1972.
Silva, T. *Psittaculture, The Breeding, Rearing and
Management of Parrots,* Silvio Mattacchione
& Co., Pickering, Ontario, Canada, 1991.
Vriends, Matthew M. *Simon & Schuster's Guide to
Pet Birds*, 5th edition, Simon & Schuster, New
York, 1989.
————*The New Bird Handbook,* Barron's Educa-
tional Series, Hauppauge, New York, 1989.

Magazines

AFA Watchbird
(American Federation of Aviculture)
Box 56218
Phoenix, AZ 85079-6218
American Cage-Bird Magazine
1 Glamore Court
Smithtown, NY 11787
Journal of the Association of Avian Veterinarians
5770 Lake Worth Road
Lake Worth, FL 33463-3299

Index

Page references in **boldface** indicate color photos. **C1** indicates front cover; **C2**, inside front cover; **C3**, inside back cover; **C4**, back cover.

Index